SELF-GUIDED
Alaska

SELF-GUIDED
Alaska

With 31 illustrations and photographs; 5 maps

LANGENSCHEIDT PUBLISHERS, NEW YORK

Publisher:	Langenscheidt Publishers, Inc.
Managing Editor:	Lisa Checchi Ross
U.S. Editorial Adaptation:	Mitchell Nauffts
U.S. Editorial Staff:	Dana M. Schwartz
Cartography:	Gert Oberländer; Adaptations by Polyglott-Redaktion and Dan McAleese
Illustrations:	Heinz Bogner
Cover Design:	Diane Wagner
Cover Photograph:	Alaska Division of Tourism
Text Design:	Irving Perkins Associates
Production:	Ripinsky & Company
Photographs:	Nos. 1, 2, 4, 7, 9, 10, 11, Karl Teuschl; Nos. 3, 5, 6, 8, Alaska Division of Tourism
Translation:	James Hogarth
Original German Text:	Karl Teuschl (author); Polyglott Redaktion (editorial)
Letters:	We welcome your comments and suggestions. Our address: Langenscheidt Publishers, Inc. 46-35 54th Rd. Maspeth, N.Y. 11378

Contents

Foreword

The Aleuts called it *Alyeska,* "the Great Land," and Alaska is truly that—and much more.

For untold millennia now, man has braved Alaska's sometimes hostile climate in order to hunt its magnificent wildlife, harvest its teeming waters, and stand in awe of its majestic scenery. The original Alaskans—Eskimos, Aleuts, and Indians—learned to adapt to its extremes of daylight and temperature and developed cultures closely tied to the rhythms of the land and sea. During the 18th century, Russians, English, and Spanish alike searched in vain for the keys that would unlock its wealth. Faced with mountains that seemed to touch the sky, rivers of ice that ribboned over the horizon, trackless forests as big as many countries, and ocean storms that turned even the saltiest tars white with fear, they eventually left the Great Land for others. Just a hundred years ago, "gold fever" drew thousands upon thousands north like lemmings, their dreams of fame and fortune a match for the uncompromising wilderness only as long as the ore held out. More recently still, the discovery of oil has sparked a second rush "north to the future," and the obstacles that Nature had spent eons preparing have been surmounted one by one.

But if Alaska has been tamed, it hasn't been conquered. And so, in the hearts and minds of would-be pioneers everywhere, it remains "the last frontier," the last place he or she can go now that the Wild West is no longer wild, now that the local swimming hole is overrun by strangers or paved over by asphalt, now that the great national parks in the "lower 48" are bumper-to-bumper with recreational vehicles from Memorial Day to Labor Day. It is the last place where the coasts and wild rivers, the forests and mountains remain largely untouched by the hand of man; nor has the climate been put under a dome. The infrastructure of civilization is—to put it simply—just not there. This, ultimately, is its allure for tens of thousands of people the world over. And while an Alaskan vacation might not be everyone's cup of tea, for those who relish adventure, love the outdoors, and get weak-kneed in the presence of soaring snow-capped mountains, crystal-clear streams alive with spawning salmon, or the sight of a half-ton moose breaking through a birch thicket to drink at a glass-smooth meadow pond, there is no place quite like it.

Chances are, if you've read this far, you already know that much of Alaska is inaccessible by car. It should come as no surprise, however, that the 49th state's three major population centers—Anchorage, Fairbanks, and the capital city of Juneau—are, in fact, connected by good highways and/or (in the case of Juneau) an extensive marine highway system. Langenscheidt's *Self-Guided Alaska* gives you three travel routes covering most of the options you will face if you decide to drive to Alaska, including detailed descriptions of the cities, towns, and historic places you'll encounter along the way. In addition, *Self-Guided Alaska* has a special section describing a number of expeditions into the Alaskan "bush"—by definition, anywhere in Alaska you can't get to by car, which means most of the state. Written especially for seasoned travelers, this unique guide gives you all the information you'll need to explore Alaska at your own pace and to follow your own interests.

Self-Guided Tours

The heart of this book is its self-guided tours. Walking tours of Anchorage, Fairbanks, and Juneau describe all the important sites in those cities and put them in historical perspective. The three driving tours take you past some of the most spectacular scenery you'll ever see. Detailed maps outline every route. A final chapter will introduce you to five towns that serve as the gateways to the Alaskan bush should you decide to make your vacation to Alaska a real adventure.

Using This Guide

This travel guide helps you plan, organize, and enjoy your vacation in Alaska. In "Getting Your Bearings," a brief rundown of Alaska's different regions and topographical features is designed to give you a feeling for the vast scale of the 49th state. A historical chronology and an essay on native arts and culture provide helpful background and perspective on the sights you'll be seeing. Alaska's three major cities are described in detail in the Travel Routes that follow this section.

Langenscheidt's writers also offer a subjective guide to the most appealing sights. Our unique three-star system appears throughout this guide:

  ***Worth a special trip—don't miss it!
  **The most important sights on the tour
  *Highlights

Total distance is provided in miles and kilometers from the departure point of each tour. Major towns and sights appear in boldface for easy reference, while other notable places appear in italics. Numbers in parentheses correspond to locations on the maps.

The guide concludes with a Practical Information chapter divided into two parts. The first is General Trip Planning, to help you gather information you'll need before you depart for Alaska. The second part is specific information—such as local tourist information offices and hotels—listed town by town.

Notes and Observations

Travel information, like fruit, is perishable. We've made every effort to double-check information in this guide. But hotels do close and roadside museums or attractions do shut down for renovation, so be sure to check ahead whenever possible.

We welcome your comments and updates of our information. Please write us at:

Langenscheidt Publishers, Inc.
46–35 54th Road
Maspeth, NY 11378

Getting Your Bearings

Location and Size

If Alaska were superimposed over the "Lower 48," with its north-ernmost point, Point Barrow, positioned on the Minnesota-Canada border, then Ketchikan, the southeastern tip of the panhandle, would fall in the vicinity of Charleston, South Carolina, while Attu Island, the western-most of the Aleutians, would find itself all the way across the continent near Yuma, Arizona.

With an area of 582,412 square miles (1,524,671 square km.), by far the largest of the 50 United States, Alaska is actually a peninsula "hinged" to the northwest corner of the North American continent along the length of its 1,538-mile- (2,475-km.-) long border with Canada. Sprawling over 1,400 miles (2,250 km.) from Point Barrow south to Amchitka Island in the Aleutians, and some 2,400 miles (3,900 km.) from Ketchikan west to Attu, Alaska is fully one-fifth the size of the other 49 states combined.

If that's too difficult to fathom, then try to imagine a state that, until very recently (September 15, 1983), encompassed *four* different time zones (since reduced to two—Alaska Standard Time, one hour earlier than Pacific Standard Time, and Aleutian-Hawaii Standard Time, one hour earlier than that), or one bounded by *two* oceans—the Arctic and the Pacific—*and* two seas—the Bering and Chukchi.

Not surprisingly, in a state of such immense proportions, Alaska is a land of superlatives. If you're looking for the outsized, chances are you'll find it in Alaska, including the highest mountain in North America (Mount McKinley); the largest glacier in North America (the Mal-aspina); the longest glacier in North America (the Bering); the most powerful earthquake ever recorded in North America (the 1964 Good Friday quake—8.7 on the Richter scale); the largest national park in the United States (Wrangell-St. Elias); the largest state park in the U.S. (Wood-Tikchik); the largest and second-largest national forests in the U.S. (Tongass and Chugach); the largest wildlife refuge in the U.S. (Yukon Delta); the world's largest concentration of bald eagles (Chilkat Bald Eagle Preserve); the northernmost city in the U.S. (Barrow, which is also the largest Inupiat Eskimo community in the world); the west-ernmost settlement in the U.S. (Adak); the largest and busiest seaplane base in the world (Lake Hood, Anchorage); the highest per capita in-come in the U.S. ($32,000); and so the list goes on. Is it any wonder that a lot of Texans seem to have suffered from an inferiority complex since Alaska became the 49th state?

Regions

Obviously, Alaska's greatest attraction for visitors is the pristine beauty of its measureless landscapes and the magnificence of its abundant wildlife. At first glance, however, Alaska just might seem too big to ever get a handle on. And while it's true you'll only be able to sample a fraction of its natural wonders and historic landmarks in a single visit, it will surely help you plan your itinerary if you think of Alaska in terms of its five different regions: Southeast, Southcentral and the Gulf Coast, Southwest and the Bering Sea Coast, the Interior, and the Arctic. Each has its own distinct history and flavor, and each will reward the visitor to Alaska with its own special variety of breathtaking scenery and adventure.

Southeast, as Alaskans refer to their spectacular "Panhandle" region, is a 500-mile- (800-km.-) long coastal strip bounded lengthwise by the Coast and St. Elias mountains to the east and the densely wooded off-

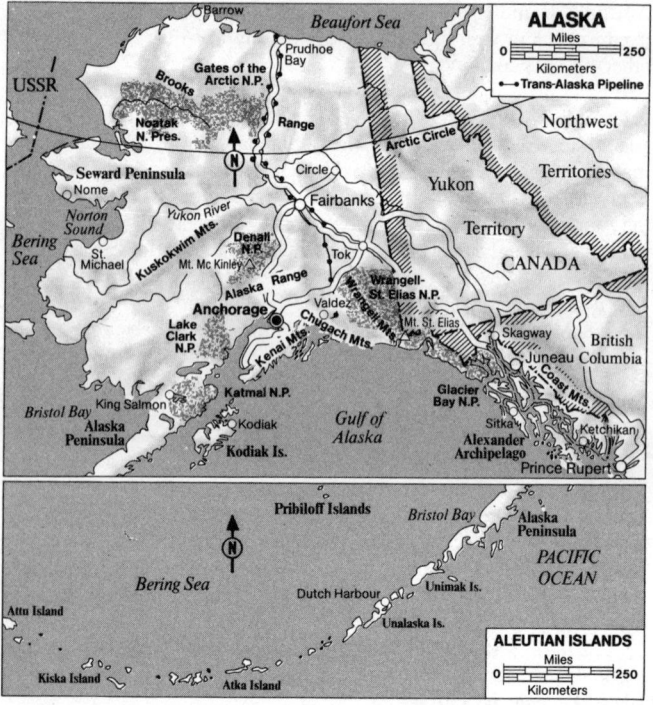

shore islands (over a thousand) of the Alexander Archipelago to the west. With the Panhandle mainland at no point more than 30 miles (48 km.) wide, and much of that slashed by countless fjords from the Canadian border in the south to world-famous Glacier Bay in the north, Southeast is a fairytale land where spruce- and hemlock-covered mountains plunge into deep-water bays, coves, and inlets at every twist and turn of the sheltered Inside Passage. Here, too, Alaska's rich and varied past is most prominently on display.

Ketchikan bills itself as the salmon capital of the world and also boasts the world's largest collection of totem poles, the unique art form of the Tlingit, Haida, and Tsimshian Indians. It's also the gateway to the *Misty Fjords National Monument,* a dramatic land- and seascape of thickly forested slopes, plunging waterfalls, and eerie mists. *Wrangell,* farther north, is the only town in Alaska to have existed under Russian, British, and American administrations. *Petersburg,* a pretty fishing village on Kupreanof Island, proudly celebrates the ancestry of many of its long-time inhabitants with the little Norway Festival every May. *Sitka,* situated on a beautiful harbor on the west coast of Baranof Island, was once the largest city on the west coast of North America and the capital of Russian America. This legacy has been lovingly preserved in its St. Michael's Cathedral and Russian Bishop's House, while its Sheldon Jackson State Museum is particularly recommended for its collection of native artifacts. Farther north still, *Juneau* perches on a narrow strip of land between the Gastineau Channel and the steep slopes of Mount Juneau (3,820 feet/1,161 meters); it is Alaska's capital, with all the amenities and conveniences that implies. When the weather clears, it is perhaps the most spectacularly situated state capital in America. The magnificent *Mendenhall Glacier* is just a short 13-mile (21-km.) trip from downtown.

Nearby *Admiralty Island* is a wildlife paradise, with the largest brown or grizzly (zoologists have determined they are varieties of the same species) bear population in the Panhandle, as well as the highest concentration of nesting bald eagles on the North American continent. Just across Chatham Strait, Chichagof Island is home to the largest Tlingit Indian settlement in Alaska at *Hoonah,* and proudly displays its close ties to the sea in fishing villages such as Elfin Cove and Pelican. Situated on the Lynn Canal, beautiful mountain-ringed *Haines* hosts the Southeast Alaska State Fair every August, while the nearby *Chilkat Bald Eagle Preserve* boasts the world's largest concentration of the magnificent birds—some 3,500—late every autumn. At the head of the Lynn Canal, *Skagway,* with its well-preserved historic Main Street district, is a popular point of debarkation for thousands of cruise ship passengers and the jumping-off point for the famed 33-mile- (54-km.-) long Chilkoot Trail—the route of expedience (if not choice) for the tens of thousands of gold seekers who poured into Canada's Yukon Territory during the Klondike Gold Rush of the 1890s. It remains a popular destination for well-conditioned hikers today.

No vacation to Alaska's Southeast would be complete without a day or overnight cruise to **Glacier Bay National Park and Preserve*, the fascinating terminus for 16 spectacular tidewater glaciers. The sights and sounds of "calving" glaciers, frolicking seals and otters, and the breaching of the endangered humpback whale are guaranteed to elicit "oohs" and "aahs" from even the most jaded traveler. At the northern end of the Panhandle, *Yakutat,* on the shores of postcard-pretty Yakutat Bay, is the gateway to the *Malaspina Glacier,* and at 1,500 square miles (3,885 square km.) the largest piedmont glacier in North America—larger than the entire state of Rhode Island.

Of course, with water the dominant element in the Panhandle region, Southeast Alaska is a water sport enthusiast's dream come true. The countless bays and coves of the Inside Passage offer abundant sportfishing opportunities, and kayakers from all over the world come every summer to paddle its hundreds of miles of deep-blue water. Hunters, too, will find game in abundance, including brown and black bears, wolves, wolverines, mountain goats, Sitka black-tailed deer, fox, and the occasional moose. Hikers willing to contend with an often soggy climate and a variety of challenging terrain can explore the hundreds of miles of trails maintained by the U.S. Forest Service in the region. There are 150 recreational cabins available for rent on a weekly basis in the Tongass National Forest. For those who prefer to keep the great outdoors at more of a distance, glacier flightseeing, whale-watching cruises, and pleasure boating are all popular activities in the Panhandle. And while paved roads are the exception rather than the rule in this region where the sea meets the mountains, the excellent and reliable Alaska Marine Highway System makes travel easy and a delightful adventure in itself.

Southcentral and Gulf Coast: Curving 650 miles (1,050 km.) from Kodiak Island in the southwest to Yakutat at the northern end of the Panhandle, the Southcentral and Gulf Coast region is "urban" Alaska—over two-thirds of the state's population lives here, with half the total residing in *Anchorage* (population 230,000). Of course, "urban" in Alaska means something far different than it does in the Lower 48. And while Anchorage has become a cosmopolitan, international crossroads (in terms of air miles, it's roughly equidistant between New York and Tokyo), much of the Southcentral region, with its roller coaster topography, is as wild and unspoiled as any destination in the remote Alaskan bush.

The most popular tourist destination in Alaska is ***Denali National Park,* the home of Mount McKinley, at 20,323 feet (6,195 meters) the crown jewel of the rugged Alaska Range and the tallest mountain in

North America (some say the world, since its gain in elevation surpasses that of Mount Everest). But the park itself is far more than just a stage for that massive, snow-covered giant. Within its nearly six million acres, most of it largely undisturbed by the hand of man, you'll encounter some of the grandest scenery and magnificent wildlife in all of North America. Best of all, Denali's splendors are readily accessible by car via the George Parks Highway and, once you've arrived at the park, from shuttle buses that take visitors into and out of the park (thereby minimizing the impact of vehicular traffic on Denali's wildlife).

The *Matanuska-Susitna* (or Mat-Su, as it's usually abbreviated) *region* south of Denali National Park and north of Anchorage is the agricultural heartland of Alaska, where good soil and 20-hour days during the short growing season combine to produce giant specimens of broccoli, cabbage, pumpkins, potatoes, and a variety of other vegetables. The busy towns in the area are surrounded by experimental farms sponsored by the University of Alaska. The Dog Mushers Hall of Fame is located in *Knik*.

Anchorage, of course, is Alaska's one true urban center, with all the pros and cons that go with it. Its setting on a point of land that juts into Cook Inlet is spectacular, its skyline undistinguished at best, and its weather surprisingly temperate for a city located at 61° North latitude. And while you'll be able to spend your money in a wide array of restaurants, shops, and boutiques while you're in Anchorage, you'll also pay for the privilege—Anchorage's cost of living is traditionally among the top three in the United States.

South of Anchorage, and connected to the mainland by a narrow neck of land, is the breathtaking **Kenai Peninsula,* a microcosm of Alaska's great natural diversity packed into 9,050 square miles (23,400 square km.)—an area about the size of Rhode Island, Connecticut, and Delaware combined. Here you'll find gorgeous mountain scenery, towns founded by Russians in the late 18th century (Kenai and Seldovia), one of Alaska's more artistically inclined communities (Homer), an ice field that dates back to the last Ice Age (the Harding Icefield), and a storm-battered coast with fjords that rival anything Norway has to offer (Kenai Fjords National Park). And, with the exception of the Kenai fjords (which are best appreciated from the comfort of a charter boat out of Seward), all of this can be accessed via the well- maintained Seward and Sterling highways.

Seward, on the Gulf coast of the Kenai Peninsula, is also the point of departure (via the Alaska Marine Highway System) for wild and wet *Kodiak Island,* the largest island in the state and the site of the first permanent European settlement in Alaska. Today the island is known for its rugged beauty, its wide-ranging fishing fleets (the city of Kodiak is one of the top three fishing ports in the U.S.), its precariously situated airport and frequent fog, and its legendary bears—the largest brown bears in the world. The *Kodiak National Wildlife Refuge* is home to the greatest density of these awe-inspiring creatures, and attracts intrepid photographers and wildlife-watchers from all over the globe.

At Portage, situated on a narrow arm of Cook Inlet at the neck of the Kenai Peninsula, you'll find the *Portage Glacier,* one of Southcentral Alaska's most popular sights. Also from here, the Alaska Railroad shuttles cars past the snow-capped mountains to *Whittier,* which is also the western terminus for the Alaska Marine Highway System's ferry runs through island-dotted *Prince William Sound.* Stretching eastward over some 15,000 square miles (38,850 square km.), the watery wonderland of the Sound was, until recently, a forgotten backwater rarely visited by anyone other than local fishermen. All that changed when Valdez, with the most northerly ice-free port in the Western Hemisphere, became the southern terminus for the Trans-Alaska Pipeline. Today, the Sound is a playground for kayakers, pleasure boaters, whale-watchers, glacier enthusiasts, hikers, hunters, and sports fishermen, as well as home to a bustling commercial fishing industry. The Chugach Mountains, which circle the Sound like a pearl necklace, serve as a barrier to the frequent storms that blow in off the Gulf of Alaska, forcing them to dump their precipitation as rain along the coast and as mind-boggling amounts of snow in the higher elevations of the mountains. The results are evident in the lush Sitka spruce and hemlock forests of the *Chugach National Forest* (at 5.8 million acres, about the size of New Hampshire) and the 20 tidewater glaciers that spill into the Sound, including the massive **Columbia Glacier.*

Travel in the Sound region is hampered by a distinct absence of roads. However, one of the few paved ones in the area, the Richardson Highway, ends at *Valdez,* a fishing village that was totally destroyed by the Good Friday earthquake of 1964 and then was reborn as the pipeline's southern terminus. Valdez suffered a major man-made disaster in 1989 when an oil tanker ran aground in Prince William Sound, befouling the pristine waters that surround the town and threatening the ecology of the area for hundreds of miles. Valdez's spectacular mountain backdrop has earned it the soubriquet, Alaska's "Little Switzerland."

The Richardson Highway heads out of Valdez and swings over *Thompson Pass* (site of the heaviest snowfall totals ever recorded in Alaska), past the *Worthington Glacier,* and connects with the rest of the Alaska Highway system at Glennallen, the gateway to the *Wrangell-St. Elias National Park and Preserve.* This is the largest national park in the United States and, along with the adjacent Kluane National Park across the border in Canada, a designated World Heritage Site. Here, volcanic activity and tens of thousands of years of the effects of grinding ice have combined to create a mountain wilderness the equal of any in the world, with 9 of the 16 tallest peaks in the U.S. Needless to say, the wildlife in the park is as spectacular as the scenery, with the usual brown and black bears, wolves, moose, and caribou thriving in the lower elevations, and sure-footed Dall sheep and mountain goats making their home among the sheer cliffs and crags of the higher elevations.

McCarthy/Kennicott, end-of-the-road for the gravel Edgerton Highway, is tucked in a valley between the St. Elias and Wrangell mountains. It is a national historic landmark, thanks to its early 20th-century history as one of Alaska's largest mining operations and scene of the world's richest copper strike. It's also a convenient jumping-off point for the many activities that can be enjoyed in the park, including backpacking, guided river trips, mountaineering, hunting, fishing, flightseeing, and cross-country skiing (in winter).

As if all this doesn't give you enough to choose from, the Anchorage area increasingly has become a destination for winter sport enthusiasts from the Lower 48. In fact, Anchorage was the choice of the U.S. Olympic Committee to host the 1994 Winter Olympics (after the International Olympic Committee decided to "split" the summer and winter games, running them in alternating biannual cycles), and most of the alpine events would have been held at Mount Alyeska, a world-class resort and ski area just 40 miles (64 km.) south of the city. Anchorage is also the start of the grueling 1,149-mile- (1,750-km.-) long *Iditarod* race, the premier sled dog race in the world, and the scene of the always interesting Anchorage Fur Rendezvous (called "Rondy" for short by the locals). The 10-day festival in February features sled dog racing, fur auctions, traditional Eskimo blanket tosses, and a wide variety of arts and crafts.

Obviously, variety is the watchword in the Southcentral and Gulf Coast region of Alaska. With all of this and more to do and see, the kind of experience you'll discover here is only limited by the amount of time you have and your own imagination.

The **Southwest and Bering Sea Coast** region embraces the 500-mile- (810-km.-) long Alaska Peninsula, the more than 200 islands of the Aleutians and Pribilofs, the huge delta formed by the mighty Yukon and Kuskokwim rivers, and the mostly treeless, arrowhead-shaped Seward Peninsula. Though too vast to be pigeonholed, it's a region characterized by great barren expanses, remote Native villages, and the presence of water everywhere. It's also a region of spectacular, if often stark, natural beauty, as well as a critical wildlife habitat and vast area of marine fisheries—a fact recognized by the tens of millions of acres here that have been put into the national wildlife refuge and park systems. Don't plan on driving in this neck of the woods, however; roads connecting its far-flung outposts are virtually nonexistent. Southwest Alaska and the Bering Sea Coast are very much a part of the "bush," and travel by private planes and small charter airlines is the rule rather than the exception.

The economic pillars of the region are commercial fishing and tourism, with most visitors attracted by its world-class salmon and trout fishing and the unsurpassed opportunities for observing wildlife and bird populations. *Iliamna,* on the northern shores of Iliamna Lake (Alaska's largest) is the gateway to the most important red (or sockeye) salmon spawning habitat in the world, and a favorite destination of fishermen the world over. It's also a convenient departure point for *Lake Clark National Park and Preserve,* a magnificent wilderness of 10,000-foot (3,000-meter) peaks, glaciers, tundra, lakes and streams, wild and scenic rivers, and a spectacular coastline on Cook Inlet. Within the park's boundaries you'll find an extraordinary variety of wildlife characteristic of Alaska, including Dall sheep at the southern limit of their range, as well as whales and seals at play in the waters of Cook Inlet.

South of the park and Iliamna Lake, the *McNeil River State Game Sanctuary* is perhaps the most famous spot in the world for viewing brown bears. During the peak season, from July 1 to August 25, Alaska Fish and Game officials escort no more than 10 visitors a day (permit required) to a lookout point above the McNeil River, where as many as 60 bears at a time wade, splash, and belly-flop about in pursuit of their favorite food, chum salmon.

At the head of the Alaska Peninsula, **Katmai National Park and Preserve* is home to more of Alaska's famed wildlife, including a large concentration of brown bears, as well as the *Valley of Ten Thousand Smokes,* an eerie and fascinating geological remnant of the 1912 eruption of the Novarupta volcano. This beautiful national park also encompasses a representative sample of the peninsula's terrain, from its mountainous and indented coastline of the Shelikof Strait (which separates the peninsula from Kodiak Island) to the lowland lakes and rivers of the Naknek watershed. *King Salmon,* the gateway to Katmai and much of the rest of the Alaska peninsula, is a typical bush community, with a number of wilderness lodges, boat and airplane facilities, stores, and a handful of restaurants and motels.

Much of the rest of the peninsula, which is characterized by forested hills and dominated by the rugged and still actively volcanic Aleutian Range, has been parceled into national wildlife refuges and/or monuments. From northeast to southwest, they are: the *Becharof National Wildlife Refuge,* the *Alaska Peninsula Wildlife Refuge,* the *Aniakchak National Monument and Preserve,* and the *Izembek National Wildlife Refuge.* Access to these wilderness areas is usually by plane from King Salmon and not inexpensive, but the rewards for the avid outdoors enthusiast cannot be exaggerated. At the same time, visitors must never lose sight of the fact that this is the bush. The weather on the peninsula is often wet and windy, and storms can blow up in a hurry, so the National Park Service advises backpackers, hunters, and fishermen on their own to plan accordingly.

Where the Alaska Peninsula ends, the 1,500-mile (2,400-km.) sweep of the Aleutian chain begins. Often described as having the worst weather in the world, the Aleutians are comprised of five major island groups numbering almost 200 islands, all of them virtually treeless and many of them actively volcanic. Lying in a great arc where the frigid waters of the Bering Sea meet the warmer waters of the Pacific, these remote islands were called "the birthplace of the winds" by the Aleuts who first settled them. Today, the population of the islands is about equally divided between Aleuts and U.S. military personnel, a by-product of the Second World War, when Japanese aggression illustrated the strategic importance of the chain to U.S. security and the majority of the Aleuts were relocated to Southeastern Alaska for the duration of the war. (Sadly, many of them chose not to return to the islands after the war's end.)

Much of the chain has been protected as part of the *Alaska Maritime National Wildlife Refuge,* a haven for millions of seabirds and waterfowl, as well as the most diverse collection of wildlife species in any of Alaska's refuges. Though often wet and shrouded in fog, the Aleutians manage to attract thousands of visitors every year who come to hike and backpack the rugged terrain (bears are not a concern here), photograph the wildlife, and, if they're bird-watchers, add to their "life lists." And on those infrequent occasions when the weather clears, the Aleutians present the lucky visitor with sweeping vistas of lonely islands adrift in the blue expanse of the Pacific. *Dutch Harbor* on Unalaska Island and *Cold Bay* at the westernmost tip of the Alaska Peninsula are the most popular gateways to the Aleutians, with direct scheduled air service from Anchorage available to both. (The Alaska State Ferry also makes periodic stops in the islands during the summer months.)

Dutch Harbor and Cold Bay are also the jumping-off points for the *Pribilof Islands,* "the Galapagos of the North," located northwest of the Alaska Peninsula in the cold waters of the Bering Sea and famous the world over for their fur seal and seabird (over 200 species) colonies. The two main islands in the group, Saint Paul and Saint George, have pleasant visitor accommodations, and each boasts a Russian Orthodox church on the National Register of Historic Places. Even farther north, *St. Lawrence Island,* just east of the International Date Line and only 40 miles (65 km.) from the Siberian mainland, is home to two communities of Yup'ik Eskimos. Visitors to the island are usually flown over on day-long tours out of Nome and given a fascinating look at the subsistence culture of the Yup'iks. The island itself has been inhabited for thousands of years and boasts four archaeological sites on the National Register of Historic Places, as well as a carefully managed reindeer population that has grown from 70 animals in 1900 to a herd of nearly 10,000 today. In addition, St. Lawrence Islanders are famous for their ivory carvings, which are sold at stores in both of the island's two towns, Gambel and Savoonga.

Back on the mainland, *Dillingham* is the gateway to the sportfisherman's paradise of Bristol Bay, the world's largest producer of red, or sockeye, salmon. In addition to the sockeye, the Bristol Bay watershed is home to large numbers of the other four species of Pacific salmon (chum, pink, silver, and king), trophy-sized rainbow trout, arctic char, graylings, and Dolly Varden trout. The area around the bay is dotted with fly-in fishing lodges, as well as a dozen or so Eskimo villages whose residents depend on the commercial fishing industry as well as subsistence hunting and fishing for their existence. Dillingham is also the departure point for *Wood-Tikchik State Park* and the *Togiak National Wildlife Refuge.* Wood-Tikchik is the largest state park in the United States (and some say the most beautiful) and offers a breathtaking variety of scenery, from rugged mountains and glacial valleys to gravel beaches and tundra. Togiak, which borders on Wood-Tikchik, preserves much of the same kind of dramatic scenery and is, in addition, a haven for migrating waterfowl.

Bethel, at the mouth of the Kuskokwim River in the southcentral part of the *Yukon Delta National Wildlife Refuge,* is the largest town on the Bering Sea Coast and its commercial center. Besides serving as the administrative center of the surrounding area, Bethel is the transportation hub for 57 Eskimo villages in the delta, many of them situated on the banks of the Yukon and Kuskokwim, Alaska's two longest rivers. The Yukon Delta Wildlife Refuge is the largest in the United States, a vast, treeless lowland of rivers, streams, and thousands of lakes and ponds covering some 19.6 million acres. The refuge protects a good deal of the most critical breeding habitat for shorebirds and waterfowl in North America, and supports a variety of wildlife besides. *Nunivak Island,* across the Etolin Strait, has become home for a large breeding herd of musk ox, transplanted there from Greenland in the 1930s after the species had been hunted to extinction in Alaska in the mid-19th century.

Travel in this boggy, roadless region can be difficult and expensive, the weather unpredictable, the insects omnivorous, and the tourist amenities few and far between, but for the avid sportfisherman, bird-watcher, or wildlife photographer, a trip to the Yukon delta region can be unforgettable.

Heading north from the delta along the shores of Norton Sound, *Unalakleet* marks the boundary between the northern limit of the Yup'ik Eskimo and the southern limit of the Inupiat Eskimo. (The Unalakleet River is also one of the best-kept fishing secrets in the state.) On the northern shores of the Sound, 550 miles (890 km.) northwest of Anchorage, you'll find *Nome,* the notorious one-time gold rush boomtown and today the gateway to the Seward Peninsula and northwestern Alaska, as well as the finish line for the grueling 1,049-mile- (1,750-km.-) long Iditarod Trail Sled Dog Race. Nome, the saying goes, never met a visitor it didn't like and is renowned for its boisterous hospitality and the excellent quality of its Native crafts, especially ivory. As most everywhere else in the bush, the fishing and wildlife viewing on the peninsula, though often hard to reach, are superb. The weather, on the other hand, is unpredictable and the region remote, so backpackers on their own should plan accordingly.

A good portion of the northern half of the Seward Peninsula has been designated the *Bering Land Bridge National Preserve,* a gold mine of a different kind. Here, archaeologists have surmised, is one of the areas most likely to have hosted animals and humans as they migrated from Asia to North America over the now-submerged land bridge tens of thousands of years ago. Today it is a starkly beautiful reminder of the unquenchable curiosity and indomitable spirit of mankind.

Interior: Bounded on the south by the Alaska Range and the north by the remote Brooks Range, and covering nearly a third of the state from the Canadian border in the east to the Yukon delta lowlands in the west, the Interior of Alaska is what generations of people with wanderlust have tried to imagine when their thoughts have turned northward. Carpeted by trackless forests of spruce, birch, and aspen; drained by great, meandering rivers such as the Yukon, Tanana, Porcupine, and Koyukuk; subject to extremes of temperature and daylight; and virtually unexplored by other white men as recently as 120 years ago—the Alaskan Interior has proved more than a match for even those with the wildest imaginations.

Today, the Interior shows signs of becoming tame, if not exactly "civilized." Fairbanks, the state's second-largest city (population 27,000), is situated in the heart of the region at the confluence of the Chena and Tanana rivers. In addition, modern, well-maintained roads such as the Richardson and George Parks highways have their northern termini there. Even more remarkable, the 416-mile- (675-km.-) long *Dalton Highway,* or *Pipeline Haul Road,* begins its snaking route to the shores of the Arctic Ocean north of Fairbanks. The suspicion lingers, however, as any "sourdough" (Alaskan old-timer) will tell you, that all this is just so much veneer on the essential wildness of the region. And the fact remains that much of it is accessible by bush plane or boat only, while great stretches of it reveal no trace of human presence.

While the rivers of the Interior were the preferred routes of travel for the Athapaskan Indians, the original inhabitants of the region, today's visitors can explore large and spectacular portions of it from the comfort of their cars and recreational vehicles. The most famous Alaskan road of all, the Alaska Highway, leaves Canada a few miles northwest of Beaver Creek, Yukon Territory, and immediately begins to follow the northern border of the *Tetlin National Wildlife Refuge.* In addition to its three roadside campgrounds, the refuge protects a variety of wildlife habitat (bears are especially fond of the area), as well as a number of geological features of interest.

Northwest of the refuge, the Alaska Highway presents the traveler with a couple of options. At Tok, the Tok Cut-Off (Highway 1, an extension of the Glenn Highway) heads southwest past the Wrangell Mountains and Wrangell-St. Elias National Park and Preserve, and eventually joins the spectacular Glenn Highway (which continues on in the shadow of the Chugach Mountains to Anchorage) at Glennallen. Though Anchorage, in theory, is only a day's drive on this all-weather highway, reality has a way of intruding in the form of severe frost heaves and pavement breaks. From Tetlin Junction, a few miles east of Tok, the 161-mile- (259-km.-) long Taylor Highway (which is closed in winter) winds its way northeast into old gold-mining country and eventually ends at the Yukon River town of *Eagle,* a gateway to the *Yukon-Charley National Preserve.* Yukon-Charley protects a 128-mile (208-km.) stretch of the Yukon River, which is wide and slow-moving through the preserve, as well as all of the wild and scenic Charley River, one of the truly pristine rivers left in the United States.

If neither of these options proves tempting, the Alaska Highway continues in a northwesterly direction toward Fairbanks and the heart of the Interior. At *Delta Junction,* an important farming community where you'll also get your first glimpse of the Trans-Alaskan Pipeline, the Alaska Highway merges with the Richardson Highway for the run into Fairbanks. You can also follow the Richardson south from Delta Junction to Valdez on Prince William Sound, a spectacular drive that takes you over or past *three* magnificent mountain ranges—the Alaska, the Wrangell, and the Chugach.

Fairbanks is to the Interior what Anchorage is to Southcentral Alaska—its commercial, administrative, and transportation center. Founded as the result of a fortuitous miscalculation, Fairbanks has survived boom-and-bust cycles and the climatic extremes of the Interior to become a flourishing city of 27,000 in the most unlikely of places—65° North latitude (few cities this far north—one in Norway and a handful in the Soviet Union—are larger). The visitor to Fairbanks can choose from a wide selection of accommodations, restaurants, and activities while there. You can then opt to head back south on either the Richardson or George Parks Highway, which skirts the eastern boundary of ***Denali National Park and Preserve*** (see *Southcentral and the Gulf Coast* section above), or choose to continue on deeper into the surrounding area.

During the long days of summer, the Steese Highway retraces the path of the early gold seekers as it pushes 162 miles (262 km.) northeast into the Interior, where it dead-ends at *Circle.* In the years immediately preceding the Klondike Gold Rush, Circle was the biggest boomtown on the Yukon River. Today, it's little more than a ghost town but it can be used as a jumping-off point for the *Yukon Flats National Wildlife Refuge,* a huge complex of wetlands, sloughs, and ponds bisected by the Yukon River (and the Arctic Circle). In addition to having one of the highest densities of nesting waterfowl in North America, the refuge sees king, coho, and chum salmon from the Bering Sea pass through it every summer—the longest salmon run in the United States. Fly-in service to *Fort Yukon,* the old Hudson's Bay Company outpost at the confluence of the Porcupine and Yukon rivers, and now the largest Athapaskan Indian community in Alaska, is also available from Fairbanks. Visitors to the refuge should remember that most of it is remote and subject to dramatic fluctuations in water levels and hordes of insects during the summer months.

Northwest of Fairbanks, the mostly gravel Elliott Highway dead-ends at *Manley Hot Springs,* a summertime resort community (with a number of year-round residents) centered around the natural springs there, and also the home of two-time Iditarod winner Susan Butcher.

For the truly adventurous, the Dalton Highway, or Pipeline Haul Road as it's commonly called, branches off from the Elliott Highway 5 miles (8 km.) north of the small community of *Livengood.* For the 255 miles (412 km.) after that, it winds its way north through some of the most remote terrain in all of North America, in the course of which it becomes the only road in the United States to cross north of the Arctic Circle. At *Disaster Creek,* near Dietrich, the road is closed for the rest of its length to Prudhoe Bay, unless you have a permit from the Alaska Department of Transportation. For those who might be tempted to check out this ulti- mate "road trip," a word of warning: the Dalton Highway was built for no-frills, long-distance hauling. Roadside amenities are virtually nonex- istent, the road itself is narrow and prone to severe heaving, and the truckers who use it often drive as if they thought it was Memorial Day at the Indianapolis Speedway. You're advised to bring your own water sup- ply, since safe drinking water is not available along the highway, and if your car breaks down, be prepared to pay a small fortune for a tow truck out of either Yukon Bridge or *Coldfoot,* 59 miles (96 km.) north of the Arctic Circle.

Bettles, south and west of Coldfoot, is headquarters for a number of outfitters/guides who take interested parties into the ancient and vir- tually uninhabited Brooks Range, the divide between the Alaskan Inte- rior to the south and the Arctic to the north. Many outdoors enthusiasts consider the wilderness experience within the Brooks Range's vast na- tional parks and preserves to be among the "purest" in the world. **Gates of the Arctic National Park,* with all 8 million of its acres lying north of the Arctic Circle, protects the headquarters of six designated wild rivers—the Noatak, Alatna, John, Kobuk, Tinayguk, and North Fork Koyukuk—and provides key habitat for 36 species of mammals, includ- ing grizzly and black bears, wolf, moose, caribou, Dall sheep, and mountain goats. Summer days are long, with a stretch of continuous daylight from late May to mid-July, and temperatures on the southern slope of the range are markedly warmer than those on the north slope. Most visitors on their own arrange to be dropped off and picked up by plane. There is one wilderness lodge (at Walker Lake) within the park's boundaries; otherwise there are no facilities within its millions of acres. In the face of such daunting isolation, visitors are warned to be self-sufficient and schooled in wilderness survival skills in the case of emergency.

South of the Brooks Range, the rest of the Interior is true bush Alaska—accessible by plane, boat, snowmobile, or dog team only; not surprisingly, a good deal of it has been placed into the national wildlife refuge system. From northeast to southwest these are: the *Kanuti National Wildlife Refuge*, the *Nowitna National Wildlife Refuge*, the *Koyukuk National Wildlife Refuge*, and the *Innoko National Wildlife Refuge*. While space constraints prevent us from giving a full description of these remote wilderness areas, a few words about each will give you an idea of what to expect.

The Kanuti Wildlife Refuge, 150 miles (243 km.) northwest of Fairbanks, encompasses parts of two river basins (the Koyukuk and Kanuti), rolling plain, and countless streams and marshes. In addition, it provides habitat for 139 species of birds, all the large Alaskan land mammals as well as a number of smaller fur-bearers, and four species of Pacific salmon, arctic char, grayling, lake trout, and northern pike. The Nowitna refuge, 200 miles (324 km.) due west of Fairbanks, is dominated by the Nowitna River, which is a designated wild river and a favorite of charter float trip outfits. The Koyukuk refuge, 320 miles (518 km.) west of Fairbanks, is home to the *Nogahabara Sand Dunes*, one of the two active sand dune fields in Alaska; much of the rest of the refuge is either lowland forest or tundra. The Innoko refuge, about 300 miles (485 km.) northwest of Anchorage, is broken up into two parcels encompassing extensive wetland areas in the central Yukon River basin. Access to it is out of *McGrath* and *Galena*. McGrath is a colorful mining town with a variety of overnight accommodations, restaurants, services, and festivals (including a Fourth of July parade, a bluegrass festival, a state fair, and the Iditarod, which passes through town every March). Galena, a former supply depot for mining operations in the area, today boasts a good-sized bush community with a large Koyukon Indian population, an advanced air base for F-15s, and a variety of tourist amenities. As in all of Alaska's wildlife refuges, camping facilities in these federally owned lands are nonexistent, the terrain is usually rugged, and the wildlife—including bears, wolves, and moose—outnumbers people. If you plan to visit one of these refuges, be prepared for a true wilderness experience and all that it implies. And *always* respect the camps, fish nets, and equipment of the local people, many of whom depend on subsistence hunting and fishing for their survival.

Arctic: Extending westward from the Canadian border to the Bering and Chukchi seas and bordered on the north by the Arctic Ocean and the south by the Brooks Range, the Alaskan Arctic was, until 20 years ago, the largely ignored preserve of the Inupiat Eskimo. All that changed in 1968, of course, when the Atlantic Richfield Company discovered a huge oil field off the Arctic coast near Prudhoe Bay; the region has been struggling to come to grips with the impact of that discovery ever since.

While the Arctic remains a largely unspoiled and fragile environment, signs of the oil boom are everywhere. The Trans-Alaska Pipeline and the Pipeline Haul Road run down the North Slope to their northern termini at Prudhoe Bay. At Barrow, the multi-story headquarters of oil companies stand side-by-side with the clapboard shacks and shanties of the town's Eskimo residents. Empty gas cans, snowmobile parts, and satellite dishes vie for space with harpoons, fish nets, and other trappings of a subsistence lifestyle. More and more, visitors from the "Outside" are showing up in Barrow and other far-flung Native villages to experience the unique beauty of the Arctic wilderness firsthand. While their intentions may be pure-hearted, the long-term effects on Inupiat culture remain to be seen.

With the exception of the southwestern corner of the region around Kotzebue Sound, the Arctic slopes gently from the crest of the Brooks Range to the Arctic Ocean and is drained by a series of rivers that run from south to north. Underlying much of this coastal plain is a layer of permanently frozen ground, or permafrost, up to a depth of 2,000 feet (600 meters). The presence of this permafrost (besides posing a major obstacle to any sort of large-scale construction project) prevents water from percolating more than a few feet below the surface of the tundra during the warmer months. The result of this phenomenon in combination with a low rate of evaporation turns the tundra into a vast bog and, near the coast, speckles it with thousands of small lakes and ponds. During its long winter, on the other hand, the combination of bitter cold and poorly drained soil results in the formation of pingoes, small hills created by up-thrusting ice. Huge expanses of tundra also break into the outlines of regular geometric patterns, an effect caused by cracks in the ice filling in with sediment during the summer months, only to be lifted above ground level as the tundra is once again plunged into the deep freeze. Yet another Arctic phenomenon is the ever-present fog, which blankets the coast much of the year, creating a navigational hazard for bush plane and helicopter pilots and a constant irritant for everyone else.

Yet despite the difficulty of travel over the tundra, the bitter cold and continuous darkness of the deep Arctic winter, and the forbidding isolation of life above the Arctic Circle, the region has been inhabited for thousands of years. Archaeological evidence of man's long history in this region has been unearthed and recently protected in the *Cape Krusenstern National Monument,* on the northern shores of Kotzebue Sound. There, extensive digs have yielded artifacts that provide a fascinating picture of the succession of early mankind in the Arctic.

The gateway to the Cape Krusenstern monument is the largely Eskimo community of *Kotzebue,* at the tip of the Baldwin Peninsula, which knifes across Kotzebue Sound. It was formed by the same combination of waves and pack ice that created Cape Krusenstern. Serviced daily by jet from Anchorage via Nome, Kotzebue is a bustling community with accommodations and amenities for visitors. It is also the headquarters for NANA, the Northwest Alaska Native Corporation, and the commercial center for the region. Kotzebue also acts as the departure point for trips to the Bering Land Bridge National Preserve (see *Southwest and the Bering Sea Coast* section below), as well as three other spectacular wilderness areas: *Selawik National Wildlife Refuge,* the *Kobuk Valley National Park,* and the *Noatak National Preserve.* Access to these remote public lands is all but limited to charter airplane, an expensive proposition this far north, and, depending on the season, infrequently by boat, snowmobile, dog team, or cross-country skis (for the truly prepared and well-conditioned).

The Selawik National Wildlife Refuge, which straddles the Arctic Circle, is best known for its extensive tundra wetlands and flocks of migratory waterfowl, as well as being a winter feeding ground for herds of caribou. There is also continuous daylight here in June and early July, as well as swarms of insects. Kobuk Valley National Park borders the Selawik refuge to the north and protects the *Great Kobuk Sand Dunes,* the largest active Arctic dune field in the world. Within the park's boundaries, Dr. J. Louis Giddings, the archaeologist who discovered the evidence of prehistoric communities at Cape Krusenstern, found evidence of human habitation dating back 12,500 years—what has been described as the most important archaeological find ever in the Arctic. Today, most visitors float through the park on the gentle Kobuk River, which has its headwaters in Gates of the Arctic National Park and Preserve (see the *Interior* section above). Backpackers frequently head north into the Baird Mountains, which serve as the divide between the Kobuk and Noatak watersheds. As elsewhere in Alaska's parks and refuges, visitors are asked not to interfere with the subsistence activities of the local Natives.

The sprawling Noatak National Preserve, like the adjoining Gates of the Arctic, is one of the truly pristine wilderness regions in the world. Cradling the mountain-ringed basin of the 400-mile- (648-km.-) long Noatak River—perhaps the most unspoiled river in North America—

the preserve's importance to the plant and animal communities of the Arctic and sub-Arctic has been recognized by UNESCO, which designated it an International Biosphere Reserve. The natural splendors within its boundaries include a 65-mile- (105-km.-) long canyon, rolling hills, tree-dotted uplands, and an extensive coastal delta. Numbering over 200,000, the western caribou herd migrates through the park and back again every April and August, and large members of bear, wolf, moose, caribou, Dall sheep, lynx, and smaller fur-bearers, as well as 125 species of birds, further enhance its reputation as an unsurpassed wilderness region. At the same time, it is one of the most remote areas in all of Alaska—you might not see a plane overhead, let alone another person, for days at a time. All visitors to the park should be self-sufficient, familiar with wilderness survival skills, and leave a copy of their itinerary behind with a friend or ranger.

North of Kotzebue and the great parks and preserves of the Brooks Range lies the vast coastal plain of the Arctic, otherwise known as the North Slope. The gateway to this surreal landscape of tundra, ice, and 24-hour daylight or darkness (depending on the time of year) is *Barrow,* the largest Inupiat Eskimo community in the world and the headquarters for the multinational concerns that are developing the oil reserves under the Arctic Ocean. Most visitors to Barrow come with package tours run out of Fairbanks or Anchorage and stay for a night or two. Activities in the area include tundra tours, fishing and hunting (although only Natives are allowed to take marine mammals), dog sledding, snowmobiling, and cross-country skiing in winter, plus trips to the sand spit at Point Barrow, the northernmost point in the United States. The scattered Eskimo villages along the coast rely on subsistence hunting and fishing for their existence and offer very little in the way of visitor amenities. Some package tours include a trip to the pipeline facilities at Prudhoe Bay for those curious to see how the impact of the huge project on the fragile Arctic environment has been minimized.

Much of the Alaska east and south of Prudhoe Bay has been protected in the *Arctic National Wildlife Refuge,* a treeless wilderness of glaciated peaks and streams and rivers flowing both north and south. Because this refuge just may be the wildest and most unspoiled of all Alaska's wilderness areas, it has become increasingly popular with outdoors enthusiasts over the last few years, attracting kayakers, river-rafters, hikers, backpackers, mountain climbers, and wildlife photographers to its 20.3 million acres.

At the same time, it has also attracted the attention of the big oil companies, who want to see it opened for exploratory drilling (many believe that an oil field with reserves as great as those of Prudhoe Bay lies there waiting to be discovered). The battle between environmentalists and oil developers is shaping up to be one of the most divisive of the 1990s, and will go a long way to determining future policy in the rest of Alaska's federally owned lands. In the meantime, most visitors to the park are flown in and out by charter plane from either Fort Yukon or Fairbanks, and are warned to be self-sufficient and well-prepared, both physically *and* psychologically, for the potential hardships of an expedition into the high Arctic. For those up to the challenge, however, the Arctic National Wildlife Refuge will provide them with a memorable wilderness vacation.

Topography and Climate

On a geologic continuum, the 49th state is still an adolescent, having only "arrived" at its present configuration some 20 million years ago. For the 500 million years or so prior to that, geologists tell us, pieces of the earth's crust were drifting about on the ocean of molten magma that surrounds the earth's core. According to the theory of plate tectonics, when these pieces, or "plates," collided, a number of things could happen. Sometimes, the plates would slide past each other along a seam, or "fault" (a process that continues today along such seams as California's San Andreas Fault, perhaps the most famous in the world). At other times, a drifting plate might be forced under a second, more stable plate in a process geologists call "subduction." This usually led to a violent deformation or up-thrusting of the top plate, and quite often, the formation of volcanoes, as sediments carried by the subducted plate were brought closer to the earth's core, where they would be turned into superheated magma and then rise back toward the surface of the earth's crust seeking an outlet.

Over tens of millions of years, these inexorable processes caused a large chunk of the North American landmass to swing out toward the Asian landmass, until the two continents were eventually joined by a broad belt of land, or "land bridge." At the same time, bits and pieces of land associated with underlying plates were sliding along faults in a northwesterly direction as the so-called Pacific plate drifted toward the North American continental plate. As these smaller plates collided with the one bearing the Asian-North American landmass they were subducted, causing massive upheavals to the top plate and triggering violent volcanic eruptions along a broad front. That, at least, is how geologists today account for the precipitous mountain ranges of Southcentral Alaska and northwestern Canada, as well as the long line of volcanic peaks that comprise the Aleutian Range. (The high incidence of earthquake and volcanic activity in this region is further evidence, geologists say, that the sliding and subducting of plates continues deep beneath the earth's surface.)

It was left to the massive ice sheets of the Pleistocene epoch to put the final touches on Alaska's magnificent landscape, however. Alternately advancing and retreating over the northern latitudes of North America during successive "ice ages," these vast sheets of grinding ice— Nature's version of the bulldozer—left behind a topographical legacy of steep-sided fjords, coastal islands, and broad basins when they retreated for the last time some 12,000 years ago. In Alaska itself, the glacial activity was more or less confined to the southern and northern portions of the state, leaving much of the Interior ice-free and open to the migrations of nomadic peoples who periodically crossed over the land bridge from Asia.

Today, the results of these awesome natural forces are dramatically evident throughout Alaska. From the towering mountains of the Coast, Chugach, and Alaska ranges, to the still-active volcanoes of the Aleutian chain, to the labyrinthine bays and channels of the Panhandle, the 49th state is a geologist's dream come true. At the same time, Alaska's spectacular geology has an enormous influence on its climate—or, more accurately, its climates. For, thanks to its mountains and the fact it's a peninsula (surrounded by water on three sides), Alaska has not one, but four different climatic zones—maritime, transitional, continental, and Arctic. What follows is a brief description of each of these zones as they relate to the five regions of the state described above.

All of *Southeast* Alaska, from Ketchikan to Yakutat Bay, falls into the maritime zone. Warmed by Pacific Ocean currents and sealed off from polar air masses by the Coast and St. Elias mountains, Southeast is characteristically damp and temperate, with average annual precipitation in the region totaling more than 92 inches (234 centimeters) (although some communities, especially in the extreme southeast corner of the state, report up to 200 inches/500 centimeters annually, so be sure to pack a raincoat). Daytime temperatures in Juneau, in the center of the region, average 55°F (13°C) in July, with an occasional high in the 70°–80°F (23°–28°C) range, while the January average is 22°F (−6°C). The driest months (a relative term in this part of the state) are April and June, with precipitation steadily increasing throughout the summer and fall (October is the Southeast's wettest month). Along the coast, you'll encounter snow on the ground intermittently from mid-November to mid-April, with rain and sleet not uncommon. The higher elevations of the Coast and St. Elias mountains receive up to 400 inches (1,000 centimeters) of snow every year, which, in turn, feeds the many glaciers that flow down their sides.

The *Southcentral and Gulf Coast* region is characterized by two climate zones, one strongly maritime and the other transitional. Stretching from and including all of Kodiak Island, the eastern portions of the Kenai Peninsula, and all of Prince William Sound and the Gulf coast to Yakutat Bay, the maritime zone is cool, wet, and subject to so-called Aleutian depressions that send storms into the Gulf capable of generating 50-foot (15-meter) waves and dumping upwards of 160 inches (406 centimeters) of precipitation annually. By no means is there a uniform pattern, however, and the amount of precipitation a community receives depends to a large extent on its location vis-à-vis surrounding topographical features. Kodiak, for example, which is not hemmed in by cloud-scraping mountains, receives about 74 inches (188 centimeters) of precipitation annually, with June and July the driest months and October the wettest. Its average daily temperature in July is 54°F (12°C), while it's a relatively mild 30°F (−1°C) on average in January. Farther north, Seward, on the eastern coast of the Kenai Peninsula, is subject to similar temperature and precipitation patterns, with heavy snowfall in the higher elevations of the Kenai Mountains (the Wolverine Glacier was, at the end of the winter of 1976–1977, the site of the deepest snowpack—356 inches/927 centimeters—ever recorded in Alaska). Once into Prince William Sound proper, however, where the Chugach Mountains act as a barrier to storms blowing in from the Gulf of Alaska, average summer temperatures are a little warmer, average winter temperatures are about 5° lower, and precipitation totals are markedly higher—from 174 inches (442 centimeters) annually at Whittier (including 264 inches/670 centimeters of snow) to 167 inches (424 centimeters) at Cordova. The combination of colder winter temperatures and higher precipitation in this region also accounts for the heavy snowfalls in the Chugach Mountains and the spectacular concentration of glaciers that spill down their sides into the Sound. (Thompson Pass, in the mountains north of Valdez, is the site of the heaviest snowfalls in a season and month ever recorded in Alaska—975 and 298 inches/2,476 and 757 centimeters, respectively.) And while it's not true that a sunny day in the Gulf Coast region is as rare as a hen with teeth, you'll be well advised to pack your rain gear if it's on your itinerary.

The Southcentral region's transitional zone extends from the crest of the Chugach Mountains north to the crest of the Alaska Range, and includes Anchorage, Alaska's largest city, and the Mat-Su river valleys, its agricultural heartland. Here, in the rain shadow of the Chugach and Kenai mountains, temperature extremes are more pronounced and precipitation totals dramatically lower. Anchorage, for example, only receives an average of 15 inches (38 centimeters) annually, while the average temperature in July is 59°F (15°C), with daytime highs frequently in the 70°–80°F (21°–28°C) range. The warmer summertime temperatures and long days in this region (Anchorage is smiled upon by close to 19.5 hours of sunlight during the summer solstice) result in a 120-day growing season in the Mat-Su river valleys, where vegetables of legendary proportions are grown. During the winter months, a warm marine current circulating around Cook Inlet and the towering Alaska

Range to the north keep Anchorage and the surrounding areas relatively isolated from the bitter cold of the Interior, with the average January temperature a bracing (and dry) 12°F (−11°C).

The *Southwest and Bering Sea Coast* region also boasts two distinct climate zones—the maritime climate of the Aleutian chain and the southeast coast of the Alaska Peninsula, and a transitional zone along the coast from Bristol Bay northward. Because of their unique situation as a barrier between the relatively warm waters of the Pacific's Japan Current and the cold waters of the Bering Sea, Aleutian weather has often been described as the worst in the world. Seemingly constant precipitation (of which there is some measurable form 200 days out of every year), fog, wind (Amchitka Island has recorded the windiest weather in the state), and fierce fall and winter storms have always made life in the Aleutians a test of resolve and fortitude. While the Japan Current and the archipelago's southern latitude moderate temperatures some—summer temperatures at Dutch Harbor range from 4°–16°C (40°– 60°F) and −2°– 3°C (28°–38°F) in winter—conditions can change in an hour, and visitors to the Aleutians are advised to dress in layers and be prepared for a variety of weather.

During the summer, the southeastern flank of the Alaska Peninsula is subject to the same type of maritime climate you'll find on Kodiak Island and throughout the Aleutians—cool, wet, and windy. On the other side of the Aleutian Range (which runs down the spine of the peninsula), however, the maritime climate gives way to a transitional zone that hugs that coast and extends from Bristol Bay northward all the way to Point Hope above the Arctic Circle. The summer temperatures in this zone are somewhat cooler than those in the crescent-shaped transitional zone between the Chugach and Alaska ranges, and average anywhere from 40°– 60°F (4°–16°C), depending on the latitude (it's generally cooler as you head north). Precipitation totals average around 20 inches (50 centimeters) annually, with most of that falling in July, August, and September. Winds sweeping in off the Pacific and Bering Sea unimpeded by dramatic topographical features are also a factor in this region, and wind chill can be much lower than the actual temperature.

During the long winter months, the climate of the Bering Sea coast begins to resemble that of the Interior more than the maritime regions, with little precipitation and extreme temperatures, especially in more northerly latitudes. Much of this is attributable to shore ice, which begins to form along the coast in October and spreads rapidly over the shallow Bering Sea, thereby negating any moderating influence it might have on winter temperatures. The average January temperature in both Bethel and Nome is about 5°F (−15°C), with monthly precipitation totals in both communities amounting to less than an inch right through May.

The Alaskan *Interior,* from the Yukon Delta east to the Canadian border, and the crest of the Brooks Range south to the Alaska Range, is subject to a continental climate noted for its great extremes of temperature and annual precipitation totals of 12 inches (30 centimeters) or less. In this region, where storms riding the prevailing winds from the south and west have to fight their way over not one but two formidable mountain ranges, stagnant air masses are common and cloud cover minimal. As a result, there is more warming by the sun during the almost continuous daylight of summer and greater cooling during the almost continuous night of winter. The average temperature in Fairbanks in June and July is 60°F (16°C), with daytime highs in the 80°–90°F (28°–32°C) range a frequent occurrence. (The all-time high in Alaska—100°F/38°C—was recorded at Fort Yukon northwest of Fairbanks in 1915.) And while thunderstorms can and do pop up on short notice, monthly summertime precipitation in the Interior averages less than 2 inches (5 centimeters), making your chances of catching good weather at this time of year better than average.

Of course, the down side to the generally delightful summer weather of the Interior is the bitter cold of a typical Interior winter. While the average January temperature in Fairbanks is only −14°F (−26°C), periods of extreme cold, with lows of −50°F (−46°C) and lower, are not uncommon. And though it doesn't snow much, what snow there is stays on the ground right through the winter. Finally, when it drops below −20°F (−29°C), there's the additional nuisance of "ice fog," a temperature-inversion-induced phenomenon that traps ice crystals, smoke, and pollution close to the ground and reduces visibility to a minimum. All of these contribute to that most Alaskan of illnesses, "cabin fever," which has been described as a "12-foot stare in a 6-foot cabin."

Given its uniqueness in every other respect, the Alaskan *Arctic* fittingly boasts a climate all its own. During the generally cloudy summer months, not even continual sunlight (there is no sunset in Barrow from May 10 to August 2) can thaw the bone-hard permafrost below a depth of more than a couple of feet, and the brisk, prevailing winds from the northeast, cooled as they sweep over the Arctic ice pack, keep temperatures from ever really warming up. While midday highs in July can climb to 60°F (16°C), they invariably fall below freezing at night. Average temperatures at this time of year range between 30°–40°F (−1°–4°C). During the long Arctic winter (which is generally clear when there's enough sunlight for it to make a difference: there's no sunrise in Barrow from November 18 to January 24), temperatures average between −1°F (−18°C) and −17°F (−27°C) from November through March, with prolonged periods of sub-zero weather.

Even though it has humidity and precipitation totals comparable to the world's deserts—Barrow receives less than 5 inches (12 centimeters) annually—the cool summertime temperatures of the Arctic inhibit the evaporation of what little precipitation does fall in the region. As a result, much of the coastal plain turns into a vast bog during the brief Arctic summer, and is carpeted by a riot of wildflowers for a few short weeks every year—always a glorious surprise for any visitor expecting to encounter an icy wasteland north of the Arctic Circle. The rainiest months in this region are July and August, with late May and early June, the best months, in terms of temperature and precipitation, for a visit.

The People

The very first visitors to Alaska, some 50,000 years ago, were nomadic hunter-gatherers from Siberia who, in their pursuit of the animals that kept them fed and clothed, crossed what is now the Bering Sea over a "land bridge"—a broad belt of land that sometimes spanned more than 1,000 miles (1,600 km.) from north to south (about the distance today from Point Hope on the northwest coast of Alaska to the western tip of the Alaska Peninsula). The land bridge gradually formed when a dramatic cooling in the earth's climate caused the creation of massive ice sheets that stretched across its northern latitudes and lowered sea levels around the globe. Over the millennia, humans migrated across this land bridge onto the North American landmass, where they then fanned out, following the ice-free river valleys of the Alaskan Interior deeper into the heart of the continent, until, in time, they reached as far as the tip of South America. Periodically, these epic migrations were interrupted as rising global temperatures caused the great ice sheets to melt, flooding the land bridge, only to be followed by another period of global cooling, a return of lowered sea levels, and the reappearance of Beringia (the name scientists have given to this land bridge). Archaeologists have determined that these profound patterns of migration and settlement finally came to an end approximately 12,000 years ago, when a significantly warmer global climate caused the land bridge to be submerged for the last time. By that point, however, much of North and South America had been inhabited and the processes of linguistic and cultural differentiation were well under way.

Migration did not end with the final flooding of Beringia, however. Some 8,000 years ago, nomads of Mongoloid stock who had developed a subsistence culture based on the hunting of marine and land mammals began to migrate across the submerged land bridge in small craft made from the skins or hides of their prey. In a relatively short period of time they had settled over the entire Arctic region, as well as the western coast of Alaska, the islands of the Bering Sea and Aleutian chain, and the coastal regions of the Alaska Peninsula, the Kodiak Islands, and Prince William Sound. In time, the southern tribes, or Aleuts, developed a cultural identity distinct from their northern cousins, the Eskimos, who in turn divided into two cultural groups of their own, the Yup'ik and Inupiat.

The *Aleuts,* who settled on the remote islands of the Aleutian chain and the rugged Alaska Peninsula, along with their relatives, the Koniag, Chugach, and Eyak, who settled in the Kodiak Islands and coastal regions of Prince William Sound, developed a culture closely tied to the bounty of the sea. For countless generations (the earliest evidence of human habitation in the Aleutians dates back some 7,000 years), the Aleuts harvested much of their food from rivers and the sea; made most of their clothing out of the skins of marine animals and the intestines of sea lions (which were waterproof); and even developed a primitive form of skis from hair-seal skins for those infrequent occasions when they traveled inland from the coast into snowier regions. To facilitate the salmon harvest, they usually built their villages near the mouths of rivers, and often entire clans would live together in large communal dwellings and share the labors and rewards of the catch. When not struggling to survive in this wind-swept and storm-battered region, Aleut men would attend to their boats and fishing equipment, which included spears tipped by hand-chiseled stone-points, weirs, nets, and stone hooks, while Aleut women would make and decorate items of clothing or weave intricate baskets of all shapes and sizes from the ready supply of rye grass that covered the islands in the summer. (Today, the grass baskets of the Aleuts, some woven so tightly that they can hold water, are treasured by collectors of Native arts around the world.)

Though far from an easy existence, it was a viable one, and the Aleut people flourished. And then (as would happen on the Great Plains of the United States some 200 years later) a more "advanced" people—in this case Russians—moved into the region and began to hunt one of its economically most important animals, the fur seal, into oblivion. It has been estimated that there were over 20,000 Aleuts in the archipelago in the mid-18th century, when the Russians made their first appearance in Alaskan waters. A century later, the fur seal was almost extinct, many Natives had intermarried or been enslaved, and the number of full-blooded and free-living Aleuts had dwindled to about 2,000, leaving the Aleutian Islands a ghostly reminder of what they had once been. As the supply and demand for furs crashed during the 19th century and Russia's territorial ambitions were focused elsewhere, the Aleut people were able to recover somewhat. However, the hostilities between Japan and the United States during the Second World War once again put Aleut culture on the defensive, and many of the inhabitants of the chain were relocated to Southeast Alaska—never to return.

Today, the Aleut people are again making a significant contribution to Alaska's diverse cultural life. The number of full-blooded Aleuts now comes to more than 1,300 and those with at least a quarter Aleut blood (thereby qualifying for the economic benefits legislated by the Native Claims Settlement Act) is close to 8,000. At the same time, their regional corporations, which were organized under the act, are active in fishing, business, tourism, and the perpetuation of Aleut cultural traditions, and the future of the Aleut people looks as bright as it has been in a long time.

If the Aleuts were the most affected of Alaska's Native peoples by the incursions of the white man, the *Eskimos*—until very recently—were the least. Protected by the trackless expanses of the Interior, forbidding mountain ranges, and an inhospitable climate, the Yup'iks of the Bering Sea Coast region and the Inupiat of the Arctic developed their subsistence culture in virtual isolation. Life in these far northern climes was hard, but, relying on fishing, hunting, and gathering, the Yup'iks and Inupiat thrived. With their villages dotting the coastline and riverbanks of the great Yukon-Kuskokwim delta, the Yup'iks depended on salmon, seal meat, and, farther inland, the occasional caribou or small mammal for their subsistence. Diets were complemented by the addition of berries in season, eggs, roots, and wild greens eaten fresh or preserved. When not occupied with the search for food or shelter, their animistic beliefs led them to carve elaborate masks that were used in their religious ceremonies. (Some of the best examples of these religiously inspired carvings can been seen at the Yugtarvik Museum in Bethel.)

Farther north, the Inupiat subsisted on whale, walrus, and seal, with the same kind of gathering activities complementing the staple items of their diet. So critical were whales to the existence of the Inupiat, in fact, that women were often tossed 20 feet (6 meters) or more into the air with the aid of animal-hide blankets in order to spot the telltale spoutings of the huge mammals beyond the shore ice—an ingenious solution to the essentially flat topography of the Arctic region (and the genesis of the "blanket toss," a popular event at most winter festivals in Alaska today).

Nothing in the austere Arctic and sub-Arctic environment was wasted, and almost everything was shared among the members of the community. The same animals that served as the basis of the Eskimo diet also provided them with clothing, tools, and a variety of other items. The skins, furs, and intestines of walruses, seals, sea lions, and small mammals were turned into trousers, boots, parkas, and waterproof garments. Bone and ivory were carved into goggles to protect the eyes from glare, knife handles, harpoon points, and fish hooks, as well as jewelry and ornamental pieces. Animal intestines were stretched to make windows for their partially buried dwellings, which were made of sod and stone and supported by whalebone or driftwood. (Contrary to popular belief, Alaskan Eskimos did not live in igloos made of snow and ice, although they sometimes built such structures in emergency situations.) Skins were also stretched over wooden frames to make drums, which were then pounded in hypnotic rhythm in accompaniment for their ceremonial dances. Life proceeded according to the seasonal cycles of Nature, and the hard-pressed but entirely self-sufficient Eskimo people developed a complex culture rich in tradition and ceremony.

Eskimo culture continues to flourish today in the small villages spread out along the rivers and tributaries of the Yukon delta and the coastlines of the Bering and Beaufort seas, as well as in the larger towns of the region such as Bethel, Barrow, and Kotzebue (the largest Inupiat community in the world). The discovery of oil beneath the Beaufort Sea, however, has inevitably subjected it to strain and conflicts. The choice for younger Yup'iks or Inupiat between the traditional methods, techniques, and lifestyles of the past and the ease and convenience of modern technology is a hard one, and not always as clear-cut as it might seem to a stranger to the culture. And while certain modern trappings have been accepted and integrated into their lives—the snowmobile and satellite dish among them—the Eskimo people remain determined to preserve as much of their cultural heritage as possible without further diluting it with the white man's often wasteful and destructive ways.

About 2,000 years after bands of hunter-gatherers from Siberia had begun to fan out along the Bering and Arctic coasts, small groups of another Native people began to appear in the river valleys of the Alaskan Interior. Related to the Navajo, Hopi, and Apache Indians of the American Southwest, the *Athapaskan Indians,* like their Eskimo neighbors to the north and west, developed a subsistence culture based on hunting and gathering in an environment that was often hostile to human activity. Benefiting from the herds of caribou that migrated through their territory in summer, and traveling by canoe along natural highways such as the Yukon, Porcupine, and Tanana rivers, the Athapaskans lived comfortably and well, supplementing their diets with salmon, rabbit, bear, moose, and berries. The harsh winter of the Interior, when temperatures might drop to $-50°F$ ($-46°C$) for weeks at a time, was another story, however; game would become scarce and travel often life-threatening. (The Athapaskans developed the art of dog mushing in response to the exigencies of an Alaskan winter.) Wearing the skins and furs of the mammals they hunted and trapped (which the women would decorate with porcupine quills and, after the appearance of Europeans in the Interior, colorful beads), small bands of Natives would retire to their isolated riverbank villages to wait out the bitter winter, surviving on fish and the occasional rabbit or weasel that strayed into their traps. Much of that time was spent in the village community house, or *kashim,* where the men worked on their tools and carving, as well as the singing and dancing that was a vital component of Athapaskan religious ceremonies, while the women attended to the details of domestic life.

Today, the largest Athapaskan community is the busy bush town of Fort Yukon, an old Hudson's Bay Company outpost situated at the confluence of the Porcupine and Yukon rivers about 150 miles (240 km.) northeast of Fairbanks as the crow flies. Here, in addition to the physical evidence of the subsistence lifestyle still pursued by many of the region's inhabitants (fish wheels, nets, trap lines, mushing paraphernalia), you'll find the Dinjii Zhuu Enjit Museum, where outstanding examples of Athapaskan art and craftwork, including birch-bark canoes and baskets, beaded moose skin accessories, and traditional tools and implements are on display. The museum is also the repository for a series of taped oral histories, some of which recount older Athapaskans' initial encounters with white men during the gold rush days at the end of the last century.

Far to the southeast, in Alaska's Panhandle region, a different kind of Indian culture began to flourish around A.D. 1000. Here, cut off from enemies by the towering heights and tangled rain forests of the Coast Mountains, three distinct Native groups—the *Tlingit* (pronounced "Klinkit"), *Haida,* and *Tsimshian*—developed an advanced culture with a rigid social order. In this narrow coastal strip, where game and seafood were plentiful and the winters relatively temperate, everyday needs could be met with minimum effort. The resulting leisure time enjoyed by these tribes, especially the Tlingit, was devoted to religion and art, most notably the art of carving. Over time, and with only a variety of stone tools at their disposal, they developed an elaborate vocabulary of stylized animal figures, which they then applied to a wide range of everyday objects, weapons, jewelry, shamans' rattles, caskets, and chests. (They were also woven into blankets made from the wool of mountain goats and cedar fibers, the famous Chilkat blankets.) Of course, the largest and most spectacular form of this artistic expression was the totem pole, for which the soft and easily split wood of the cedar proved a perfect and abundant medium.

The term *totem pole* is somewhat misleading, however. The first white men to gaze upon these strange-seeming monuments in the early 19th century interpreted the demonic-looking animal figures to be totems—supernatural beings to whom the various tribes paid religious homage. And although the name stuck, it has since been proven that totem poles have no religious significance whatsoever, but instead reflect the myths and genealogies of various family groups: they are heraldic records, or archives, of family history. In fact, with a little imagination and patience, you might be able to identify some of the figures that are used, even though they're often signified by stylized bits and pieces. A bear, for example, can be recognized by its broad jaws, numerous teeth, and hanging tongue; two large incisors and a cross-hatched tail represent a beaver; a large dorsal fin characterizes the killer whale. Other animal figures frequently encountered include the wolf, salmon, frog, eagle, and raven (which in the mythology of many tribes, Eskimos as well as Indian, was often considered to be a creator figure).

It is more difficult to identify human figures, who often appear in animal form, or mythical beings, who may incorporate the attributes of different animals. Where only a side or rear view is shown it may be impossible to make anything of the figure, as is also often the case without a detailed knowledge of a tribe's unique mythology and history. A totem pole may record anything from an old family myth to the acts of a specific individual to such natural and man-made calamities as floods, migrations, and wars. Each such event or occasion demanded its own kind of pole. A mortuary pole, for example, was erected to honor a dead notable of the tribe; a memorial pole served to commemorate a famous man or war; house poles stood at the corners of the rectangular long-houses that belonged to each extended family; and "shame" poles were designed to throw scorn on a tribe or individual who had behaved in a bad or cowardly manner.

The completion of a totem pole was always the occasion for a large *potlach,* or feast, at which the insignia and heraldic signs on the pole would be acknowledged by the other members of the tribe. In this way the privileges and accomplishments of a particular family, of which the pole was a record, were legitimized afresh. In return, the family giving the potlach was expected to distribute presents—oil, blankets, clothing, jewelry, weapons, even slaves. And once a pole had been carved, painted with vegetable dyes, and erected, it stayed up until it rotted away. Totem poles were never repaired, since this would involve a second expensive feast: instead, it was a sign of prestige (and good fortune) to commission a new pole if the first one became worn or overshadowed by some new family exploit.

In the 19th century, the metal tools introduced by white men initially led to a fresh flowering of Southeast Indian culture. The art of carving was perfected, the totem poles grew in size, and the detailing became richer and more precise. Soon, however, this contact led to a decline: disease, a new dependence on money and resulting poverty, and the destruction of traditional social structures promoted by white missionaries brought most tribes in the region to the verge of extinction. Over the latter part of the 19th century and the beginning of the 20th century, the craft of carving was ignored and the soft cedar totem poles quickly rotted in the damp Panhandle climate. If it hadn't been for anthropologists, who managed to rescue a few hundred poles in the 1930s (most of which were shipped to museums), the cultural devastation of the Southeast Indians would have been complete. Fortunately, in the years after the Second World War, a new generation of Indian artists began to revive this forgotten art of their fathers and grandfathers, rebuilding on old traditions while developing new styles and forms of their own. Today, the creative results of the newfound Native awareness and self-confidence are evident throughout Southeastern Alaska, providing an immeasurable contribution to the state's cultural diversity, as well as a reminder that the "right" way includes and respects all ways equally.

While the Spanish and, to a lesser extent, the Portuguese were wresting control of South and Central America from their indigenous peoples in the 16th century, followed by the French and British in North America in the 17th century, Alaska's Native peoples remained isolated and undisturbed. However, this changed when Vitus Bering appeared off the coast of Alaska in the middle of the 18th century. Bering's expedition of discovery was followed by those of English, French, and Spanish navigators, all of whom were motivated by a desire to find the fabled Northwest Passage between the Atlantic and Pacific oceans. When these voyages proved in vain, however, only Russia, with Pacific ports of its own, deemed it economically feasible to try to colonize Alaska. For the next hundred years or so, from its discovery by Bering and his lieutenant Chirikof in 1741 to its sale to the United States in 1867, the Russian presence in Alaska, while a small one in terms of numbers, was large in terms of its impact. Settlements of trappers, hunters, and traders were established throughout the Kodiak archipelago and islands of Southeast Alaska, and a veneer of civilization was imposed on what, until then, had been a wilderness. Russian adventurers explored great stretches of the rivers that led into the Interior, providing the first reliable information about the region's geography and economic potential. At the same time, in their rush to exploit this potential, the fur seal was hunted to near extinction and the Native people were treated with ruthless disdain.

After its sale brought an end to the Russian era in 1867, Alaska was more or less ignored by its new owners, the people of the United States, for the next three decades. Occasionally, an enterprising businessman or down-on-his-luck prospector would head north to make or find his fortune. Gold strikes were made near Sitka in 1872, Windham in 1874, and present-day Juneau in 1880. The first salmon canneries were opened in the Panhandle in 1878. It wasn't until the decade of the 1890s, however, that the inhabitants of the Lower 48 realized that their "icebox" to the north was, in actuality, a treasure chest. In short order, the discovery of gold at Circle City (1893), the Kenai Peninsula (1895), the Klondike region of the Yukon territory (1897–1900), and Nome (1898) paved the way for a frenzied stampede northward of fortune-seekers. Skagway, at the top of the Inside Passage, boomed overnight in 1897 after gold was discovered in the Yukon, growing from a sleepy Indian village of a few hundred inhabitants to a "metropolis" of 20,000 in a matter of weeks. Remote Nome experienced similar explosive growth in the summer of 1900.

The feverish influx continued when gold was found in 1902 near present-day Fairbanks. Towns began to dot the Interior, and railways and roads were built as the search for the earth's riches continued unabated. The first Alaskan oil was produced near Katalla on the Gulf coast in 1902. A telegraph line was strung from Eagle to Valdez later that same year. A giant copper strike was made near Kennicott in the Wrangell Mountains in 1910, and production began the following year. By 1916, copper had surpassed gold as the pillar of Alaska's economy. In the Panhandle region, a number of fishing villages were homesteaded by an influx of Scandinavians eager to capitalize on the rich fisheries of the Gulf, and by 1920, fishing had surpassed copper mining as Alaska's economic mainstay. Logging of the dense forests of the Southeast began in earnest in the early 1920s after a pulp mill was built near Juneau, and the Depression led to the establishment of the Mat-Su agricultural colony in 1935. All of these activities contributed to the steady growth of Alaska's population, and by 1940, the number of non-Natives, or "sourdoughs," had surpassed that of Natives, at a ratio of 40,000 to 32,500.

The Second World War brought people north to Alaska in record numbers. At the height of the conflict in the Pacific, there were over 150,000 military personnel in the future 49th state—a number that was scaled back to approximately 20,000 (where it stands today) by 1946. The 1950 census revealed a total population of 112,000, more than double that of ten years earlier, and a good indication of what lay ahead.

Today, swelled by the discovery of huge oil reserves under Prudhoe Bay in the late 1960s and the construction of the Trans-Alaskan Pipeline in the 1970s, the population of Alaska (13 percent of which is comprised of Native peoples) exceeds half a million people—a figure that still amounts to less than one person per square mile. What it lacks in density, however, it more than makes up for in diversity. The "typical" Alaskan you meet today might be anyone from an Inupiat Eskimo, who hunts whales and walruses from the traditional *umiak* (a skin-covered boat) and then returns home to watch an evening's worth of international television programming pulled in by his satellite dish, to a petite blue-eyed blonde who trains huskies for a living. He or she might be a government lawyer in Juneau, a gallery owner in Homer, a Norwegian American fisherman from Petersburg, or a Native artist from Ketchikan. Whoever they are and whatever they do, however, most Alaskans share a few traits: a stubborn desire to cling to their independence, a passion for the outdoors, and the gritty fortitude necessary to survive the harsh Alaskan winters. (In fact, Alaskans have a term—*cheechako,* a Chinook Indian word meaning "greenhorn"—for those individuals from the Lower 48 who have yet to experience this last treat.) The combination of these qualities in the people who live in the Great Land all but guarantees that the Alaskans you meet will be as unforgettable as the vacation itself.

The Economy

Furs and gold, Alaska's chief sources of wealth in the 19th and early years of the 20th century, have been relegated to a position of relatively minor importance to its economic health today. Instead, oil, commercial fishing, tourism, timber harvesting, construction, and government-sector employment have become the linchpins of a robust Alaskan economy. And while the pace of economic activity has slowed in recent years, the outlook for the 1990s is generally considered promising.

Since the imposition of the 200-mile fishing limit in 1978, which restricts foreign vessels from fishing within 200 miles (320 km.) of Alaska's coastline, the Alaskan salmon catch has nearly doubled and the commercial fishing industry, traditionally the keystone of the state's economy, has thrived. By 1985, Alaska's fish production had reached a value of $591 million annually, the highest of any of the 50 states, and was second overall (to Louisiana) in terms of volume (1.1 billion pounds). In addition, with 90 percent of the catch taken from the Gulf of Alaska and the waters of Bristol Bay, Kodiak had become the second leading U.S. fishing port (after New Bedford, Massachusetts) in terms of value, while Dutch Harbor in the Aleutians and Port Moller on the Alaska Peninsula had climbed into the top 25. The only causes for concern in an otherwise healthy industry were the king crab fishery, which remained mired in a stubborn slump, and the pink salmon catch of 1988, which dropped dramatically from an expected 40 million fish caught to an actual 12 million—a decline that caused industry spokesmen and conservationists alike to question the driftnet fishing practices of Japan, Korea, and Taiwan in the North Pacific. (The driftnets employed by these three countries, used to catch squid for the consumer market, are monofilament nets up to 35 miles/56 km. long. They are left free to drift over large expanses of ocean, snaring whatever happens to get tangled in them, including porpoises, salmon, and steelhead trout.) Additional concerns were raised in the spring of 1989 following the massive oil spill into the rich marine waters of Prince William Sound from the Exxon tanker *Valdez*, which struck a reef and ran aground southeast of the shipping channel leading out of Valdez harbor. Although the final tally for the damage done to this vitally important estuary and the subsequent losses incurred by Alaskan fishermen was still being calculated, the consensus was that the effects of the spill would be felt for years to come.

In the latter part of the 1980s, declining fortunes and the actions of Japan (specifically as an importer of unprocessed logs) were also casting a pall over the timber industry, another traditional pillar of the Alaskan economy. Although more than a third of Alaska's 336 million acres are forested, good quality timber has always been confined to the dense coastal forests of the Panhandle region. There, large quantities of western hemlock and Sitka spruce are processed by eight major sawmills, thirty-six smaller mills, and a number of pulp factories in the Sitka and Ketchikan areas. In 1986 alone, the value of Alaska's forest product exports was $255 million, accounting for over 20 percent of the state's total revenue. Exports in this sector of the economy, however, had been dropping at an annualized rate of 10 percent since 1980. The shipment of unprocessed logs to Japan, which had partially offset this steady decline, was coming under attack by conservationists and members of Congress, who expressed concern over the rapid cutting of virgin timberlands in Alaska and the Pacific Northwest, as well as the loss of jobs in the industry to automation.

For the moment, the oil industry continues to be the star performer of the Alaskan economy, as it has been for the last 15 years. In fact, ever since 1968, when a 300-million-year-old underground basin between Prudhoe Bay and Barrow was discovered by geologists of the Atlantic Richfield Company, the measure of Alaska's wealth has been calculated in terms of barrels—11 *billion* barrels, to be exact (give or take a few million). It is the largest oil field ever discovered in North America and, today, the source of approximately 80 percent of the state's revenues. Since the completion of the Trans-Alaska Pipeline in 1977, Prudhoe Bay oil has propelled Alaska into the number-one position among oil-producing states. It achieved this distinction in 1988, after running second to Texas for five years. Oil has catapulted Alaska into the modern world, financing much of its burgeoning infrastructure, swelling its population some 30 percent, and endowing it with the largest public trust fund—the Permanent Fund—in the nation.

The construction of the pipeline itself is already the stuff of legend. In 1974, after long negotiations had led to the Alaska Native Claims Settlement Act of 1971 (which paid a total of $962.5 million and 40 million acres to Alaska's various Native groups, a settlement that was to be administered by 13 Native-owned regional corporations, with a fourteenth added since) and satisfied the concerns of environmental groups, the Alyeska Pipeline Service Company went to work. All that winter, supplies were shuttled to depots north of the Yukon River, and construction of a supply road (the Dalton Highway) from Fairbanks to Prudhoe Bay was begun—a road that was eventually finished in only 154 days. That summer, the heavy road-building machines bogged down continually on the soggy Arctic tundra and workers were plagued by hordes of blood-thirsty mosquitoes. During that winter and the next, pipeline welders working in temperatures that frequently dropped below $-58°F$ ($-50°C$) suffered severely from frostbite, and in the long months of darkness above the Arctic Circle, some of them ran amok. From 1973 to 1976, over 21,000 men and women worked around the clock on the pipeline. In the same period, the population of Fairbanks nearly doubled; the roughnecks, fast-buck artists, prostitutes, and entrepreneurs attracted to the Far North by pipeline wages that averaged between $1,200 and $1,800 a week gave the place a honkytonk boomtown atmosphere reminiscent of the heady days of the gold rush at the turn of the century. Of course, there was an air of added urgency to all this frenzied activity due to the Arab oil embargo of 1973. The whole gigantic enterprise, difficulties and logistical nightmares notwithstanding, was completed in a little over two years at a cost of approximately $9 billion. On June 20, 1977, the first crude oil entered Pump Station No. 1 at Prudhoe Bay, and five weeks later, on July 28, it reached the Marine Terminal at Valdez, on the shores of Prince William Sound, where it was loaded on a supertanker and shipped south to the Lower 48. (By law, North Slope oil cannot be exported.)

Today, the Trans-Alaska Pipeline runs for 800 miles (1,280 km.) from Prudhoe Bay to its southern terminus at Valdez, crossing the Brooks Range, the mighty Alaska Range, and the heavily glaciated Chugach Mountains in the course of its journey. It runs underground for almost half that distance. Some 78,000 stilts support the pipeline above the permafrost for the remaining 435 miles (700 km.) course—a design necessitated by the fact that the pipeline, carrying oil heated to a temperature of 160°F (65°C), would otherwise sink through the partially thawed ground during the short Alaskan summer. Ten pump stations spaced along its length keep the oil flowing southward on its zigzagging course, and a 24-hour watch on the whole spectacular enterprise is maintained by helicopter, computer, and satellite.

Alaska's future as a major oil-producing state is by no means certain, however. Since the first oil entered the pipeline in 1977, production has settled at around 2 million barrels a day. A recent report estimates that half of the Prudhoe Bay field has already been pumped through it; at the present rate of consumption, the field will be totally depleted by the middle of the 1990s. With a scenario similar to that in mind, the Reagan Administration initiated competitive bidding on leases in the National Petroleum Reserve during the early 1980s—a move that was contested bitterly by environmental and Native rights advocacy groups. In the years since then, a number of companies, including Conoco, ARCO, Exxon, Shell Western, and Standard Alaska, have discovered oil and gas under the Beaufort Sea west of Prudhoe Bay. However, extraction and delivery costs are high, the market price of a barrel of oil remains relatively low, and the environmental and legal issues continue to go unresolved—at enormous expense to both sides. Slumping oil revenues have led some state legislators to call for an end to the annual dividend checks sent to every Alaskan courtesy of the State's Permanent Fund. Inevitably, a slowdown in oil exploration and drilling has contributed to a net loss of jobs and population in the state over the last four years.

On a brighter note, government-sector employment remains stable, tourism is booming, and coal and mineral mining have bright futures if their environmental impact can be minimized and accessibility to deposits is improved. According to statistics provided by the Department of Labor, the three levels of government in Alaska—local, state, and federal—employed the greatest number of people of any sector of the Alaskan economy—almost 70,000 in 1986—a trend that will more than likely continue as long as there is a Permanent Fund to administer. At the same time, tourism has become the third-largest industry in the state (after oil production and commercial fishing), and is growing at an annual rate of roughly 10 percent. The true potential of the mining industry in Alaska (with the exception of precious metals such as gold and platinum) has only been scratched, and much of the activity to date has been confined to exploration and definition of resources. Although there are huge deposits of coal west of Anchorage, molybdenum east of Ketchikan, and copper, lead, zinc, and barite in the Brooks Range, more intensive mining continues to be hampered by the inaccessibility of deposits and depressed prices for most minerals on the world market. Nevertheless, while its contribution is modest today, the next upturn in Alaska's economic development, traditionally a boom-and-bust affair, could very well be driven by the extensive mining of these valuable resources.

While the per capita income of Alaskans ($28,000) is still the highest in the nation, the figure is somewhat deceptive due to the state's high cost of living and relatively high rate of unemployment (10 percent). Even the unemployment statistic is misleading, aggravated as it is by the seasonal nature of many traditional Alaskan occupations, as well as the transient nature of a good-sized segment of the population, which, at an average age of 26, is the youngest in the United States. As a matter of course, the Alaska Department of Labor recommends to anyone planning on making their visit to the state an extended one that they have their own financial resources for support, or check out their employment prospects beforehand, or make sure they have a friend they can stay with—it's a long walk back from Anchorage or Fairbanks to the Lower 48.

Chronology

Early History

50,000–10,000 B.C.: Nomadic tribes of hunter-gatherers from Siberia cross into present-day Alaska over a land bridge that forms, disappears, and re-forms across what is now the Bering Strait during successive ice ages. The end of the last Ice Age, caused by rising global temperatures some 12,000 years ago, dramatically raises the level of oceans everywhere and submerges the Bering land bridge for the last time.

6000 B.C.–A.D. 1000: Nomads of Mongoloid stock in pursuit of marine mammals—the early Inuit—cross the Bering Strait in small craft and proceed to settle over the entire Arctic region as far east as present-day Greenland. By 500 B.C. they have developed the so-called *Dorset culture,* which gradually evolves into the *Thule culture* by A.D. 1000, though there are few linguistic or cultural differences between the two. The exceptions are the Alaskan Eskimos, whose language and customs are shaped by a way of life dependent on salmon fishing, and the so-called Mackenzie Delta Inuit of the Canadian interior, whose existence is tied to the migrations of the vast herds of caribou.

A.D. 1000: The southeast coast, or "Panhandle," of Alaska is settled by Tlingit, Haida, and Tsimshian Indians. Isolated from interior tribes by the impenetrable forests and towering peaks of the Coast Mountains, and favored by an abundant food supply, they develop a highly refined social hierarchy and advanced culture centered around villages of several hundred inhabitants.

Development of the *Aleutian culture* occurs farther north and west, along the shores of Prince William Sound, Kodiak Island, the Alaska Peninsula, and the Aleutian chain. Surrounded by the teeming marine life of the Gulf of Alaska and Bering Sea, yet constantly menaced by earthquakes, volcanoes, gale-force winds, and treacherous seas, the Aleuts eke out an existence as fishermen who rarely venture more than a mile (1.5 km.) inland.

At the same time, from the shores of Cook Inlet into the vast reaches of the Interior, Athapaskan-speaking tribes (including the Koyukon, Tanana, and Tanaina) believed to have come from Asia with the last wave of migration some 10,000 years earlier, develop the *Northern Athapaskan culture.* Living under extreme climatic conditions, these nomadic hunters follow the herds of caribou, occasionally resorting to a semi-nomadic life of fishing and berry gathering.

1000–1700: The three main groups of Alaskan native peoples develop their respective cultures in complete isolation from the influence of European culture, trading over a large area with Siberian natives across the Bering Strait and Indians from the Pacific Northwest.

The Age of Discovery

1728: Vitus Bering, a Dane sailing for Peter the Great of Russia, sights what is now St. Lawrence Island southwest of the Seward Peninsula, and sails through the strait that now bears his name.

1741: On a second expedition to the North Pacific, Bering lands off the southeastern coast of Alaska, on what is now Kayak Island; a second crew commanded by his lieutenant, Alexei Chirikof, sails farther south and weighs anchor off what is now Prince of Wales Island in the Alexander Archipelago.

Over the next three decades, Bering and Chirikof are followed by a small army of Russian fur hunters who ply Alaska's coastal waters, hunting the sea otter almost to extinction and virtually enslaving the Aleuts.

1774: Juan Perez, sailing for Spain from its New World colony of California, explores the waters off southeastern Alaska.

1776–1778: The ubiquitous Captain James Cook, in search of the Northwest Passage, explores much of coastal southern Alaska, at one point heading all the way up the 200-mile- (320-km.-) long inlet (which now bears his name) to the site of present-day Anchorage.

1784: Gregori Shelikof, a Russian fur merchant, heads an expedition that establishes a settlement at Three Saints Bay on what is now Kodiak Island.

1785– 1786: French scientist and explorer Jean François de Galoup de la Pérouse is commissioned by King Louis XVI to explore the northwest coast of North America. De la Pérouse makes landfall at Lituya Bay on what is now the western coastline of Glacier Bay National Park, but perishes on the return journey home. However, his detailed map of the bay and its five surrounding glaciers becomes the basis of comparison for all subsequent observations of these glaciers.

1791: A Russian businessman by the name of Alexander Baranof takes over management of Shelikof's Kodiak Island settlement.

Another Spaniard, Alessandro Malaspina, also in search of the Northwest Passage, strikes land in the vicinity of what is now Baranof Island and continues in a northerly direction to Yakutat Bay. Though he fails to find the fabled water route to the Atlantic, he does discover one of the largest glaciers in North America, which today bears his name.

1791–1794: The English navigator George Vancouver, following in his countryman Cook's wake, explores much of coastal southern Alaska and northwestern Canada. Near the head of Cook Inlet in 1794, he spots "distant stupendous mountains covered with snow"—most likely the first recorded sighting of the Alaska Range and its crown jewel, Denali, or Mount McKinley.

Russian America

1799: Alexander Baranof builds Fort St. Michael, with the help of 1,000 Aleuts and 100 Russians, on the site of present-day Sitka. After it is destroyed by Tlingit Indians three years later, Baranof returns to the site and rebuilds the fort, calling it *Novaya Archangelsk,* or New Archangel. By 1808, it has become the capital of Russian America and can lay claim to being the largest city on the west coast of North America.

1821: Fearing competition, especially from Great Britain's Hudson's Bay Company, the Russian-American Company (founded by Shelikof's heir, Nikolai Rezanof) pressures the czar to prohibit trading in Alaskan waters by all other nations.

1824: A treaty is signed setting the boundary between Russian America and British Canada (essentially the same one honored by the United States and Canada today), effectively ending further Russian expansion into the North American continent.

1824–1842: Russian exploration of the Alaskan interior leads to the discovery of the Kuskokwim, Nushagak, Yukon, and Koyukuk rivers.

1847: The Hudson's Bay Company establishes Fort Yukon deep in the Alaskan interior near the confluence of the Porcupine and Yukon rivers.

1848: The first mining for gold is begun on the Kenai Peninsula.

1853: Russian trappers discover the first traces of the oil that underlies Cook Inlet.

1853–1856: Having watched the profits of the Russian-American Company fall during the 1840s and early 1850s, and increasingly strapped by the financial demands of the Crimean War, the Russian government decides to give up its presence in North America.

1859: Baron Eduard de Stoeckel, Russian ambassador to the United States, is given the go-ahead to negotiate the sale of Alaska to the U.S. Negotiations are suspended with the outbreak of the American Civil War.

1867: Secretary of State William H. Seward, concluding the negotiations begun eight years earlier, convinces Congress to authorize $7.2

million—about 2¢ an acre—for the purchase of Alaska. "Seward's Folly" is immediately decried by those who think the money would be better spent reconstructing the war-ravaged South.

Gold Rush Days

1872: Gold is discovered near Sitka and then Wrangell in the Panhandle, but fails to trigger a boom.

1880: Two prospectors by the name of Joe Juneau and Dick Harris discover gold along the Gastineau Channel near the site of present-day Juneau; this time the rush is on.

1891: The first oil claims are staked out in the Cook Inlet area.

1896–1897: Word of a major gold strike on Bonanza Creek, a tributary of the Klondike River in Canada's Yukon Territory, begins to reach the "Outside"; a few months later, the steamship *U.S.S. Portland* arrives in Seattle carrying a ton and a half of gold ore. In short order, 30,000 out-of-work farmers, laborers, merchants, and speculators—squeezed at home by the economic conditions that will soon lead to the Panic of 1897—stampede northward in the great Klondike Gold Rush. Skagua, a peaceful Indian settlement at the head of the Lynn Canal, becomes Alaska's largest city, home to some 20,000 gold-crazed inhabitants; its name is soon Anglicized to "Skagway."

1898: Word reaches Skagway and the Klondike goldfields that another strike has been made in the hills around Nome in remote northwestern Alaska; within months, Skagway is all but deserted.

1902: Gold is discovered near present-day Fairbanks, which helps to establish that city. The first Alaskan oil production begins at Katalla, just north of Kayak Island.

1905: With the decline of the fur trade and the rise of the gold rush boomtowns, the territorial capital is moved from Sitka to Juneau.

1906: Peak gold production year; Alaska is granted a nonvoting delegation to the U.S. Congress.

1911: Copper production begins at Kennicott in the shadow of the Wrangell Mountains.

1912: The United States Congress votes Alaska official territorial status; the first territorial legislature is convened the following year.

1914: President Woodrow Wilson authorizes construction of the Alaska Railroad from Cook Inlet to Fairbanks; Anchorage gets its start as a tent city for railroad construction workers.

1916: The first bill proposing Alaska statehood is introduced into Congress; peak copper production year.

1923: The Alaska Railroad is completed; President Warren G. Harding is on hand to drive in the final spike.

1935: The Matanuska Valley Colony, a New Deal agricultural relief project located north of Anchorage, is founded. In time, the region will become Alaska's breadbasket, famed for the giant specimens of a variety of vegetables it produces.

The Second World War

1940: In response to increased U.S.-Japanese tensions, Fort Richardson is established at Anchorage and construction is begun on that city's Elmendorf Air Base, as well as on bases at Sitka, Kodiak, Fairbanks, and Dutch Harbor on Unalaska Island in the Aleutians.

1942: Spurred by the Japanese bombing of Pearl Harbor, the U.S. government (with Canada's approval) builds the two-lane Alaska-Canada Highway in just eight months—one of the great engineering feats of the 20th century.

June 1942: Japanese forces attack Dutch Harbor, and occupy Adak, Kiska, and Attu islands at the westernmost end of the Aleutians. In later years, American historians will decide these were diversionary feints designed to draw U.S. naval forces away from their impending encounter with the Japanese navy near Midway atoll—in retrospect, one of the deciding battles of the war in the Pacific.

June 1943: After two and a half weeks of fighting, American troops drive the Japanese from Attu. Japan loses approximately 2,570 men—an estimated 98 percent mortality rate. The U.S. loses 549 men and suffers 3,280 casualties. When the grim statistics are finally tallied, it proves to be the second most costly battle (after Iwo Jima) in the Pacific relative to the number of troops involved.

1950: Thanks in part to the lingering effects of the U.S. military presence, Alaska's infrastructure is greatly improved and the 1950 census reveals a territorial population of 112,000—50 percent greater than the previous census ten years earlier.

Alaska to the Present

1953: An oil well is sunk near Eureka, on the Glenn Highway, marking the start of Alaska's recent oil history.

1957: Oil is discovered under the Cook Inlet near Kenai.

June 30, 1958: The Alaska statehood bill is passed by the U.S. Senate. Alaska officially becomes the 49th state on January 3, 1959, after President Dwight D. Eisenhower signs the statehood bill, which includes a provision setting aside 103,500,000 acres of land for public use. William A. Egan is elected its first governor.

March 27, 1964: The Good Friday earthquake—at 8.7 on the Richter scale (a force 10 million times that of the atomic bomb dropped on Hiroshima) the most powerful ever recorded in North America—rocks Anchorage, the coastal areas of Prince William Sound, the Kenai Peninsula, and Kodiak Island. The earthquake and resulting tidal wave cause 131 deaths and an estimated $380–500 million in property damage.

1968: The Atlantic Richfield Company announces the discovery of a gigantic oilfield under the Arctic Ocean near Prudhoe Bay—a strike later verified at 9.6 billion barrels, one of the largest known oilfields on earth. When the auctioning is over, Alaska has collected a 20 percent down payment on $900 million in oil leases.

1971: Congress passes the Alaska Native Land Claims Settlement Act, granting Alaska's native peoples title to 40 million acres of land and $962 million in return for their surrender of all aboriginal claims. Thirteen regional corporations are established to administer the settlement, with any individual able to prove at least one-quarter Alaska Indian, Eskimo, or Aleut blood entitled to 100 shares of stock in his or her respective regional corporation.

1970–1973: Plans for an oil pipeline from Prudhoe Bay to Valdez on the Gulf of Alaska are delayed by lawsuits brought by various environmental groups. Pipeline legislation is finally signed by President Richard M. Nixon on November 16, 1973.

1974–1977: Over 21,000 workers flock to Alaska to work on the pipeline—an even greater engineering feat than the Alaska-Canada Highway. The first oil from Prudhoe Bay enters Pump Station No. 1 on June 20, 1977, and reaches the Marine Terminal at Valdez—a journey of 800 miles (1,280 km.) —five weeks later. After it becomes fully operational, 1.9 million barrels flow through the pipeline daily.

1978: The 200-mile (320 km.) fishing limit, which prohibits foreign vessels from fishing in Alaska's waters without a permit, goes into effect; President Jimmy Carter signs a bill withdrawing 56 million additional acres of land to create 17 new national monuments in Alaska.

1979: The state of Alaska files suit to halt the withdrawal of the 56 million acres of land by President Carter under the Antiquities Act.

1980: The Alaska state legislature repeals the state income tax, refunds all 1979 state taxes, and establishes the so-called Permanent Fund, which is designed to share a quarter of the state's oil and mineral revenues with its citizens in annual dividend checks.

Congress passes the Alaska Lands Act, placing 53 million acres into the national wildlife refuge system, 43 million acres into the national park system, 3.3 million into the national forest system, and parts of 25 rivers into the national wild and scenic rivers system.

1981: The state legislature votes to put a constitutional amendment limiting state spending on the ballot.

1982: Annual oil revenues for the state fall for the first time since the opening of the pipeline; the first Permanent Fund dividend checks of $1,000 are mailed to every resident who has lived in the state at least six months.

1984: The state of Alaska celebrates its 25th birthday.

1985: Anchorage receives the bid of the U.S. Olympic Committee for the 1992 Winter Olympics. The 1,000-mile- (1,600-km.-) long Iditarod Sled Dog Race from Anchorage to Nome is won by a woman, Libby Riddles, for the first time.

1986: The Iditarod is won again by a woman, Susan Butcher of Manley.

1987: Susan Butcher wins the Iditarod again, the third straight year a woman has won the world's premier sled dog race.

1988: Libby Riddles regains her title as winner of the Iditarod.

Alaska makes world news headlines when an international effort is made to free three gray whales trapped under the ice in Point Barrow; the three week rescue attempt, involving the Alaska National Guard, an ice-breaking vessel from the Soviet Union, native Alaskans, and environmentalists, ends in success.

1989: The worst oil spill in U.S. history occurs when an Exxon oil tanker runs aground in Prince William Sound, off Valdez, with devastating effects on the ecology of the area.

Anchorage

Situated on a flat, triangular-shaped basin at the northern end of Cook Inlet, where there was impenetrable wilderness only 80 years ago, Anchorage is a typically modern American city of a quarter of a million people—half of all the people who call Alaska home—in an atypical location—61° North latitude, or just 400 miles (640 km.) south of the Arctic Circle. Blessed with a superb natural setting—it's bounded on the west by the waters of Knik Arm, an extension of Cook Inlet, and the towering, snow-covered Chugach Mountains to the east—and a deceptively temperate climate, Anchorage manages to rise above its shortcomings (count unimaginative architecture high among them) to surprise visitors with its urbanity in the midst of such wild and sprawling grandeur.

In Alaska's "big town," as it's sometimes ambivalently referred to, you'll discover a bustling city with two daily newspapers, two four-year universities, a symphony orchestra, a lively theater arts scene, an abundance of nightclubs, restaurants, and lodging accommodations, and, of course, unparalleled ease of access to some of the most magnificent wilderness areas in all of North America. Not surprisingly, this latter attribute is one of the city's biggest drawing cards—as the many canoes in backyards, fishing rods, and hiking boots in car trunks, and miles of bicycle and cross-country ski trails within the city limits attest to. As a visitor you should know that these days most Anchorage residents are young, affluent, and outdoors-oriented. On summer weekends you'll find them driving south to the unspoiled lakes, streams, and mountains of the Kenai Peninsula, heading east to the watery wonderland of Prince William Sound, or taking off into the majestic wilderness of the Alaska Range. If they stay home, chances are it's because they play on one of the metropolitan area's 350 softball teams or have decided to "confine" their activities to nearby 495,000-acre Chugach State Park, one of the largest and most spectacular state parks in the nation. In winter, the park is a magnet for winter sports enthusiasts (although park rangers warn that the steep-sided Chugach Mountains are prime avalanche country), while thousands of downhill skiers drive the 40 miles (64 km.) south to Mount Alyeska, Alaska's largest ski resort and the U.S. Olympic Committee's choice for the 1994 Winter Games. Two other wintertime favorites are the annual Anchorage Fur Rendezvous (or "Rondy," for short), a 10-day extravaganza held in February that includes everything from sled dog racing to Native crafts shows, and the festive start of the world-famous Iditarod Trail Sled Dog Race in March.

History

The history of Alaska's largest city is a 20th-century affair, although the first inhabitants of the broad "bowl" between Knik and Turnagain Arm were Eskimos who settled there about 900 years ago, according to the archaeological record. At some indeterminate point in the centuries that followed, these Eskimos were driven from the spot by Tanaina Indians, an Athapaskan tribe. The Tanainas were also on hand in 1778, when the British navigator James Cook sailed up the long inlet that today bears his name in search of the Northwest Passage. (One version of history also has him sailing into the southern extension of the inlet and discovering there was no way out, at which point he ordered his first mate to "turn again," thereby giving that stretch of water its name, Turnagain. Cook, however, thought it was a river; it was left to George Vancouver, another peripatetic Englishman, to survey it correctly.) After Vancouver and his crew left, the basin at the head of the inlet slipped back into obscurity until the United States bought Alaska from Russia in 1867 and gold was discovered 21 years later at Crow Creek, the first non-Native settlement in the area.

It wasn't until a number of more productive gold strikes were made in the Interior, however, that Anchorage was truly born. In 1914, the U.S. government moved to build a railroad from Fairbanks to the ice-free port of Seward on the Kenai Peninsula. A decision was made to locate the construction headquarters for the project near the anchorage at the mouth of Ship Creek on Cook Inlet. In a few short months, the site had bloomed into a frontier-style tent city, and a year later its population swelled to about 2,000 (where it stayed until the eve of the Second World War). Although the immediate area around the settlement had little in the way of minerals or precious metals to help boost its economy, its fortuitous location enabled it to benefit from most of the economic developments to sweep through Alaska in the next 60 years. In 1917, for example, the offices of the Alaska Railroad were moved to Anchorage from Seward. Then, in 1935, it became the base for the federally sponsored agricultural colony in the Matanuska Valley (although its chief business remained the railroad). Five years later, with the outbreak of hostilities in Europe, Congress authorized spending for the construction of two military bases on the outskirts of town in the event of war with Japan. By the end of the Second World War, Fort Richardson and Elmendorf Air Base had been completed, and the population of Anchorage had grown to some 40,000 people. Within that same period, in 1942, the completion of the Alaska Highway in just eight months opened large parts of Southcentral Alaska and the Interior to automobile travel. Between 1957 and 1961, the discovery of oil underneath Cook Inlet further spurred the growth of the city, as well as launching what would soon become the most important sector of the Alaskan economy. Anchorage was riding high once again in the 1970s, when the construction of the pipeline brought a flood of people, booming economic activity, and un-bridled optimism to what was, by then, the most important city in the state.

Today, Anchorage continues its tradition as the commercial and trans-portation hub for the whole of Alaska, as well as the headquarters for the big banks and oil companies that have more recently transformed the frigid, inaccessible North Slope into the United States' premier oil-producing region.

The traces of the devastating earthquake that hit Southcentral Alaska on Good Friday, 1964—an earthquake that registered 8.7 on the Richter scale, the strongest ever recorded in North America—have all but disap-peared under a carpet of high-rise office buildings and housing develop-ments. The quake destroyed most of Anchorage and literally wiped out a dozen villages dotting the coastal arc of the Gulf of Alaska, leaving in its wake a city more determined than ever to join the ranks of the United States' leading cities. In fact, Anchorage's location midway between New York and Tokyo on a Great Circle route gives it a leg up on its competi-tion, which is one of the reasons why the local chamber of commerce has taken to calling the city the "Crossroads of the World." And while it can't yet threaten to unseat London, Paris, Milan, or New York as the epitome of urban sophistication—moose and bears wandering into backyards and disrupting traffic are still a common occurrence—the visitors who arrive expecting to find rude log cabins, grizzled sour-doughs, and endless nights with nowhere to go will be pleasantly sur-prised by what they find here.

Attractions

See map on page 46.

Downtown Anchorage is generally defined as the area west of Merrill Field to Knik Arm, and south of Ship Creek to Chester Creek. Many of its government buildings, cultural activities, and better hotels are located in an area of downtown bounded by Third Avenue to the north, Sixth Avenue to the south, Resolution and Elderberry parks to the west, and A Street to the east. The city sights can be seen on foot in less than half a day.

Start your tour at the **Log Cabin Visitor Information Center** (F Street and Fourth Avenue), a sod-roofed cabin typical of many of the structures erected by gold seekers, trappers, and traders who came to Alaska in the last century, and to-day an information center run by the Anchorage Chamber of Commerce. Staffed year-round by volunteers, they'll be happy to provide you with a map of the city, as well as advice on the best way to see and enjoy it. Right next door is *Old City Hall* (now the Alaska Pacific Bank), with its memorial to Secretary of State William H. Seward, the man who engineered the purchase of Alaska back in 1867 (and was roundly criticized for his folly for the rest of his days). Two other buildings in the neighborhood, the *Old Federal Building and U.S. Courthouse* and the *Fourth Avenue Theater* (which was the city's chief cultural pavilion until the new Performing Arts Center opened in 1988), are on the National Register of Historic Places.

From the log cabin, turn left onto F Street and head north (down the hill) toward the *Alaska Railroad Depot* (First Avenue opposite the tracks) and *Ship Creek,* an important source of the city's water supply. At Second Avenue, turn left again; here, you'll come across a number of Anchorage's oldest homes, including no. 542, the *Andrew Christensen House;* no. 605, the *Leopold David House;* no. 610, the *William Edes House;* and no. 618, simply called *Cottage 23.* Turn left again on Christensen Drive and follow it to Third Avenue, where you'll turn right and head west toward the water.

At the corner of Third Avenue and L Street is **Resolution Park** [1], one of the best spots in the city to view some of the soaring peaks of the Alaska Range on a clear day: Mount McKinley and Mount Foraker (17,400 feet/5,300 meters) to the north, and volcanic Mount Spurr (11,070 feet/3,375 meters) and Mount Susitna (4,396 feet/1,340 meters), the "Sleeping Lady," to the west across Cook Inlet. The park is also home to the *Captain Cook Memorial,* featuring a handsome statue of that greatest of all English navigators looking out toward his most beloved home, the sea.

Signpost

From Resolution Park, head south on L Street to Fifth Avenue. (Fifth Avenue, running one-way west, and Sixth Avenue, running one-way east, are extensions of the beautiful Glenn Highway, which takes travelers north and east toward the Alaska Highway.) To your left and down a block you can't help but notice the three gold-colored towers of the *Hotel Captain Cook,* probably the finest (if not the handsomest) accommodation in the state, which is owned by former Secretary of the Interior Walter J. Hickel. At Fifth and L Street itself is the *Alaska Wildlife and Natural History Museum,* Alaska's newest museum and a fun way to get acquainted with some of the larger examples

of Alaskan wildlife (don't worry: they're stuffed).

At the end of Fifth Avenue is *Elderberry Park,* with its wonderful views of Knik Arm and the mountains to the west, and, at its northeastern corner, the *Oscar Anderson House,* a restored two-story frame house that is the oldest structure of the city. After you've had your fill of spectacular scenery, head east on Fifth Avenue past the Hotel Captain Cook to the *Holy Family Cathedral,* at the corner of H Street; this was one of the places visited by Pope John Paul II on his layover in Anchorage in 1981.

The brand-new *Performing Arts Center,* with its three theaters and a full schedule of cultural events, is located on the northwest corner

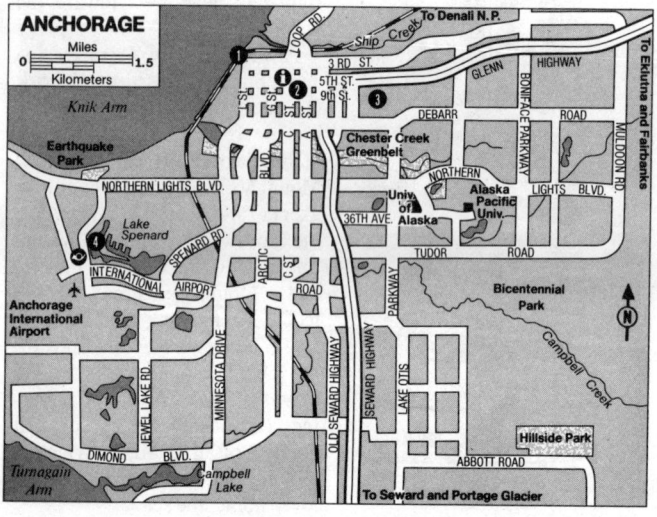

of F Street and Sixth Avenue, while restful *Town Square* (a good place to recharge your batteries) is just across the street. For those with the energy, we recommend heading south on F Street until you come to *Delaney Park*—or the "park strip," as the locals call it— a block-wide, mile-long (1.5 km.-long) outdoor mall with skating rinks, tennis courts, gardens, and a variety of other attractions. (The pope celebrated an outdoor Mass here on his visit.)

If you make it to the park strip, head east until you reach the end, then turn left on A Street, the city's geographical dividing line (streets west of A Street are designated B–U; streets to the east are also arranged alphabetically, but with full names, starting with Barrow and Cordova and ending at Orca). The entrance to the **Anchorage Museum of History and Art** (121 W. Seventh Avenue) [2] is at the corner of Seventh Avenue. The museum itself boasts Alaska's finest collections of Native arts and historical artifacts, as well as the best collection of contemporary Alaskan art anywhere.

From the museum it's a short walk north on A Street, west on Fifth Avenue past the recently completed *William A. Egan Civic and Convention Center* (named for the first governor of the state), and north again on F Street to the log cabin information center and the start of your tour.

If you decide to save the loop to Delaney Park and the museum of art for another day, head north from Town Square for two blocks to the starting point of the tour.

A number of other points of interest in Anchorage are best visited by car (they're also accessible via the city bus system, called the "People Mover" here). Just one mile (1.5 km.) east of downtown, for example, is **Merrill Field** [3], a busy facility that serves as the base for over half the licensed pilots in the state (in 1984, its 300,000-plus take-offs and landings made it the 15th-busiest airfield in the nation; it has since fallen out of the top 25). About 5 miles (8 km.) southeast of the downtown area (a 10-to-15-minute drive) are *Anchorage International Airport* and **Lake Hood** [4], one of the city's many recreational areas and the site of the busiest seaplane base in the world.

North of Lake Hood on the shores of Knik Arm is *Earthquake Park,* where a special exhibit of photographs and diagrams gives the interested visitor a good idea of the tremendous force of and destruction caused by the Good Friday Earthquake. From the entrance to the park, it's a quick drive east on Northern Lights Boulevard to Spenard Road, the city's traditional "entertainment" corridor. While people still joke about the exotic nature of some of the establishments lining Spenard, it is where most locals go for a moderately priced meal or to bend elbows with friends and other thirsty souls.

East of Spenard is **Midtown,** a

growing business and restaurant district between Chester Creek to the north and the airport road to the south. On the east, it's bounded by the Seward Highway, which leads south to Portage Glacier and the Kenai Peninsula. (It ends in downtown Anchorage, where, as Ingra Street, it runs one-way north, and as Gambell Street, runs one-way south.)

East of the Seward Highway, the Anchorage bowl opens up as you head toward the imposing summits of Chugach State Park. Here, suburban housing developments and condominium complexes alternate with large swaths of public parkland. Two of the largest are *Far North Bicentennial Park,* a 5,000-acre tract that's a favorite with cross-country skiers, snowmobilers, and dog mushers, and *Russian Jack Springs Park,* which boasts its own cross-country ski trails (including 3 miles/5 km. of lighted trails), as well as a nine-hole golf course complete with Astroturf greens. (Elmendorf Air Base and Fort Richardson each has its own 18-hole golf course, both of which are open to the public.) Nestled in between these two parks in pleasantly wooded surroundings are Anchorage's two four-year universities, the *University of Alaska/ Anchorage* and *Alaska Pacific University.*

Finally, the **Alaska Zoo** (O'Malley Road off the Seward Highway), in the southeastern portion of the bowl, is open year-round and features Alaskan animals almost exclusively, including moose, musk ox, and brown, blue, and black bears. It's also a sanctuary for orphaned or injured animals being rehabilitated for release back into the wild.

Excursions

See map on pages 54–55.

*Portage Glacier (53 miles/85 km. southeast of downtown Anchorage on the Seward Highway.) This route, which leads to the most visited attraction in the state, follows the Seward Highway (and Alaska Railroad tracks) along the northern shores of Turnagain Arm, with *Chugach State Forest* serving as a spectacular backdrop. On the way you may be able to witness a bore tide, an amazing natural phenomenon caused by great tidal movements (check with the Anchorage Visitor Information Center for tidal times). In this funnel-shaped extension of Cook Inlet, where the difference between high and low tides may be up to 39 feet (12 meters)—the greatest difference in North America outside of the Bay of Fundy—swift-moving flood tides sometimes meet ebb tides as they're still running out of the arm, with the result being a curling wave, or bore, that can crest as high as 6.5 feet (2 meters). A word of warning, however: the mud flats left behind at low tide may look inviting, but they're often nothing more than quicksand. The tide here does come in with breathtaking speed—on occasion, even helicopters have not been able to rescue trapped stragglers before it comes in. It's best to watch the show from one of the many turnouts along the way.

An access road at *Girdwood,* 37 miles (60 km.) from downtown Anchorage, leads to the base of *Mount Alyeska* (3,940 feet/1,201 meters), Alaska's biggest downhill ski resort. Skiers (many of them Japanese; the resort is owned by a Japanese consortium) are greeted by a 2,800-foot (853- meter) vertical drop, five chair lifts, a rope tow, and a pony lift, as well as hundreds of acres of above-tree-line skiing. During the summer, a chair lift takes visitors to the Skyline Restaurant at an elevation of 2,350 feet (740 meters) for splendid views of the mountains and the waters of Turnagain Arm.

At the head of the inlet, a short access road leads to *Portage Lake,* which is framed by wooded green hills and dotted by bizarrely shaped blue-white icebergs. At the far end of the lake, **Portage Glacier* grinds to a halt after its long run down from the mountains—in good weather one of the prettiest picture-postcard scenes in all of Alaska. There's an information desk in the *Begich, Boggs Visitor Center* (named in memory of two U.S. congressmen who perished in a plane crash in this area in 1972) where Forest Service naturalists will be happy to answer questions. In addition, self-guided as well as range-led hikes are both popular options here. (Note: there's no way to reach the foot of the glacier without mountaineering gear.)

*Eklutna, 25 miles (40 km.) northeast of Anchorage on the Glenn Highway, is a tiny Indian village (population 25) with a Russian Orthodox church and Siberian prayer chapel, both made out of logs. The nearby Indian graveyard is famous for its "spirit houses"—brightly painted little wooden houses that sit over the graves of the deceased, whose spirits, according to Indian belief, live in them. The small Russian Orthodox community in the village maintains the graves as well as the church; the chapel was built just a few years ago.

On the way back to Anchorage, time permitting (although we strongly recommend it), take the

Indian graveyard, Eklutna

exit for Eagle River Road, which takes you through the pleasant bedroom community of the same name in the direction of Chugach State Park. At the end of this scenic 12.5-mile- (20-km.-) long road (all but the last 2 miles/3 km. of which is paved), you'll come to the *Chugach State Park Visitor Center*, with its grand views of the mountains and excellent wildlife displays. To the east is nothing but wilderness, home to grizzlies, wolves, moose, Dall sheep, and a dozen other species of mammals—and all of it just a few miles from Alaska's largest city. The trailhead for the Old Iditarod-Crow Pass trail system is back down the access road a short distance, and a day's hike will take you to many of the glaciers in the park's interior.

***Denali National Park (234 miles/376 km.; see also pages 57–61). Although this most spectacular of national parks is easily accessible by car or recreational vehicle on the well-maintained George Parks Highway, one of the most enjoyable ways to get to it is via the Alaska Railroad, which operates daily express runs from Anchorage to Fairbanks, and vice versa, with stops at Denali, from the end of May to mid-September.

From Anchorage, the friendly-looking blue-and-yellow trains chug their way north through the glaciated valleys of Southcentral Alaska and arrive at *McKinley Park Station*, the main entrance to the park, in a little over six hours (check with the Anchorage visitor information center for departure times and fares). In the old days, the train used to stop for everyone and anyone who flagged it down, regardless of where they happened to stumble upon the tracks, which led to some excruciatingly long runs to Fairbanks and back. Nowadays, the "local" only runs once a week during the summer.

For those who feel like spending a little more money for some added luxury, the Alaska Railroad offers the *Midnight Sun Express*, two elegantly appointed high-domed cars attached to the regular express train that allow passengers to relive the glory days of rail travel as a landscape unsurpassed in North America slips by on the other side of the window. (A warning for visitors to Denali hoping to stay overnight: during the peak season from the end of May to September, early booking of accommodations is an absolute must. Call your travel agent or check with the Alaska State Division of Tourism for additional information.)

Three Travel Routes in Alaska

To many, visiting Alaska represents the challenge of venturing out into the last frontier on earth, where one can set foot where no man—or woman—has gone before. While this may be an exaggeration these days, it's not too far from the truth. At the very least, visitors to Alaska can say that they've covered territory that relatively few have had the pleasure to explore.

In a land so vast that it's almost incomprehensible, some may be overwhelmed trying to plan an itinerary that will satisfy their curiosity about Alaska in the limited time they have to spend here. To help, we offer the following three Travel Routes, designed for seasoned travelers, through Alaska's more accessible regions, as well as a section on Bush Alaska for the most adventurous wayfarers.

Travel Route 1 is a round trip excursion of the southern and southeastern regions. Originating in Anchorage, it goes north to Fairbanks, east to Tok, then drops south toward Prince William Sound before returning to Anchorage. Optional side trips and routing alternatives overland and by ferry are included along the way. We suggest a minimum of 10 days to enjoy this trip.

Travel Route 2 takes you south from Anchorage to the magnificent Kenai Peninsula with its breathtaking mountains and fjords. We suggest four days for the round trip; however, you may want to build in a few extra days to take a canoe trip on the Swanson and Moose rivers.

Travel Route 3 explores the southeastern coastal region using the extensive Alaska Marine Highway System. Alaska's spectacular panhandle, dotted with islands, slashed by deep fjords, and pierced by lofty mountains, is known the world over for dramatic Glacier Bay National Park. Because of travel time by car and ferry, and the distance involved, you should probably figure on a minimum of 10 days to explore the high points of this tour.

The section on Bush Alaska takes you to five remote Alaskan towns, where amenities are few but opportunities for adventure are as rich as the scenery. Accessible by air from Anchorage or Fairbanks, the towns serve as gateways to some of the state's vast, unspoiled wilderness areas. Unless you are a very well-seasoned wilderness adventurer (and even if you are), we recommend you join an organized group to explore these isolated reaches.

No matter where you go in this great land—the road less traveled or the one least traveled—you'll encounter nature in its purest state, with scenes so perfectly composed they may not seem real—but they are. This is Alaska.

TRAVEL ROUTE 1: Southern and Central Alaska: Anchorage–***Denali National Park– Fairbanks–Tok– *Valdez–(Whittier–) Anchorage (1,135 miles/1,825 km., or 887 miles/1,428 km.)

See map on pages 54–55.

Just three generations ago, the mighty rivers of Alaska's interior were still the primary routes of transportation in an otherwise inhospitable region that was more than twice the size of Texas. Apart from Indians, Eskimos, and a handful of fishermen of Russian descent, only a few widely scattered prospectors and trappers lived in this vast wilderness. In the intervening decades, great changes have shaped Alaska. Today, good paved roads lead to even the smallest settlements in the southcentral part of the state, and thanks to the oil industry, agriculture, and tourism, Anchorage and Fairbanks have grown up to become modern cities.

Despite the changes and growth, however, Alaska is still primarily a land of magnificent natural beauty that enthralls hundreds of thousands of visitors each year. Near the beginning of this route, in Denali National Park, North America's highest peak, Mount McKinley, serves as a breathtaking backdrop to tens of thousands of acres of spectacular sub-Arctic tundra. The route continues north from the park to Fairbanks, a one-time gold mining boomtown that survived the inevitable end of the rush, only to see itself boom all over again when a different kind of gold— "black gold," (crude oil)—was discovered in enormous quantities under the waters of the Beaufort Sea. From Fairbanks, the route then turns toward the southeast and the long forested valley of the Tanana River, which skirts the northern flank of the skyscraping Alaska Range and is fed by a dozen smaller rivers that issue from those perpetually snow-covered heights. At Tok, the route swings to the southwest and follows the Tok Cut-Off to the Richardson Highway. At this point it begins to wind its way south over the heavily glaciated Chugach Mountains to the beautifully situated town of Valdez, the southern terminus of the Trans-Alaska Pipeline. Valdez is also a popular departure point for day-long cruises to the spectacular Columbia Glacier and Prince William Sound. For those with the time and energy to do some pre-planning, you can return to Anchorage from Valdez via the Alaska Marine Highway System, which runs regularly scheduled ferries through Prince William Sound to Whittier, at its westernmost edge. From Whittier, it's a short journey under the Chugach Mountains by car-train to Portage, and another hour's drive or so along the shores of beautiful Turnagain Arm to Anchorage. For those who would rather take the more direct route, you can take the Richardson Highway north from Valdez to Glennallen, where it connects with the serene Glenn Highway, and from there it's a day's drive through the Matanuska Valley, Alaska's most important agricultural region, back to Anchorage.

You should allow at least 10 days for this round trip. If you decide to do some hiking in Denali National Park or take a side trip into the Yukon Territory (among the many options available), you will, of course, need more time. We suggest you try to work in a side trip to the Kenai Peninsula, either at the beginning or at the end of this tour, whether to fish, canoe, hike, or simply soak in the gorgeous scenery (see pages 79–80).

For a closer look at **Anchorage** (population 250,000), see the description beginning on page 42.

Leave Anchorage on the *Glenn Highway* (Highway 1), which runs in a northeasterly direction along *Knik Arm,* the northern extension of Cook Inlet. About 13.5 miles (22 km.) outside of Anchorage, you'll pass the exit for Eagle River Road and *Chugach State Park* (see page 50). At the 26-mile (41-km.) mark from Anchorage, you'll come to the Eklutna Road exit, which takes you to the village of **Eklutna* (see page 49). Ten miles (16 km.) beyond Eklutna, at the head of fjordlike Knik Arm, the *George Parks Highway* (Highway 3) branches off from the Glenn Highway and begins its run into the Interior. This is the heart of the Matanuska-Susitna farming region, which is usually abbreviated to the **Mat-Su region.**

The glacial valleys of the *Sus-*

itna River, which flows south from the Alaska Range into Cook Inlet, and the *Matanuska River,* which empties into the inlet from the east, have developed into Alaska's granary and vegetable garden, thanks to their fertile soil. During the Great Depression of the 1930s, the federal government resettled 202 impoverished farm families in these valleys, and after considerable difficulty, a thriving agricultural community was established. With help from biologists at the University of Alaska, who developed new, hearty varieties of grain and vegetables better able to cope with the rigors of the climate, giant specimens were soon being grown in spite of the region's relatively short growing season (about 120 days). Today, cabbages weighing up to 80 pounds are the pride of the Alaska State Fair, which is held every year at the end of August in *Palmer,* one of the two commercial hubs of the Mat-Su. Located on the Glenn Highway a few miles east of its junction with the George Parks, Palmer began life as the base for the Matanuska Valley Colony, the original agricultural project. Now it's a charming town of 2,800 peo-

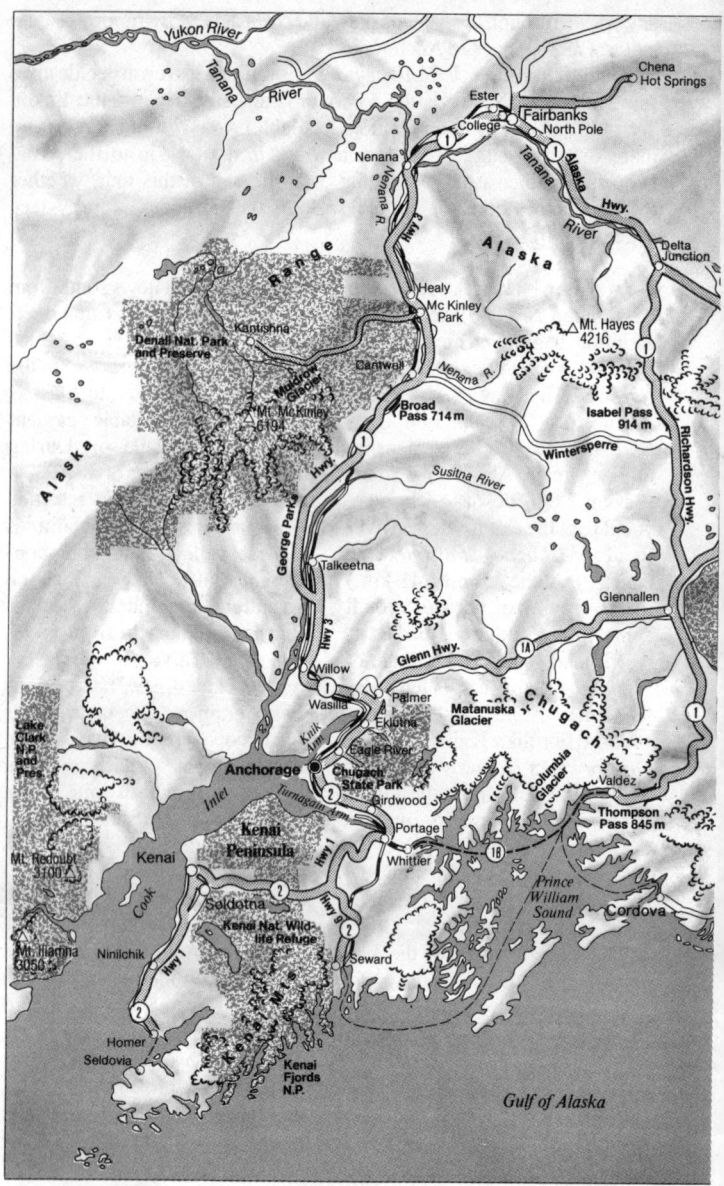

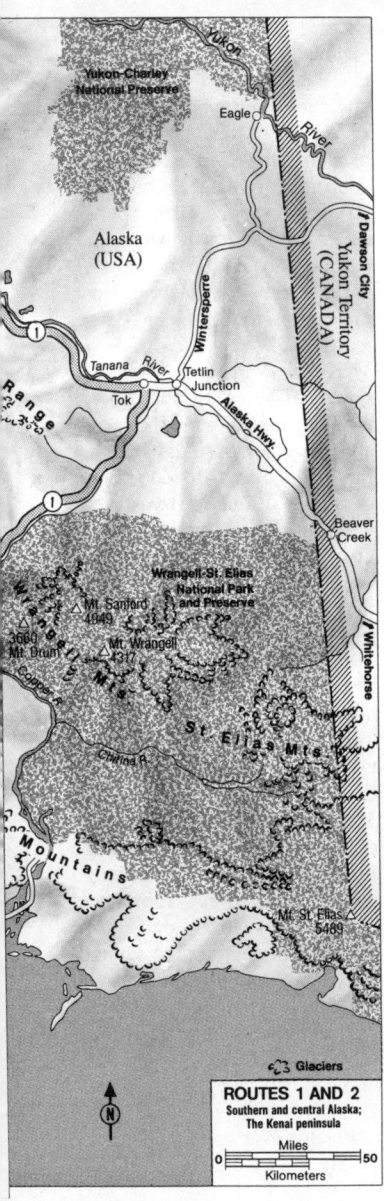

ple with a number of dining and lodging options, and enough things to see and do to occupy the better part of an afternoon. The *University of Alaska Agricultural Experiment Station* is located on the hill just past the junction of the two highways. Guided tours are offered daily from June 1 to September 1, and don't forget to take a look at the gigantic vegetables and astonishingly large flowers while you're there.

Seven miles (12.5 km.) past the junction, you'll come to **Wasilla** (population 4,000). Once upon a time it was a tiny mining village, but it has blossomed into the Mat-Su's other hub (it's the largest town on the George Parks Highway between Anchorage and Fairbanks), as well a fast-growing suburb of the big town. With its pleasant climate and picturesque location between *Lake Lucille* and *Lake Wasilla*, it's easy to see why the town has become so popular. For those with a special interest in the Iditarod (the self-styled "Last Great Race on Earth"), Wasilla is home to its headquarters (open five days a week, year-round). For the truly devoted (all you Jack London fans), a 14-mile (22-km.) detour south to *Knik*, on the northern shores of Knik Arm, will lead you to the *Knik Museum and Sled Dog Mushers Hall of Fame* (open Wednesday through Sunday, June 1 to September 15).

From Wasilla, the highway quickly leaves all suburban surroundings behind and enters a great expanse of forest. The *Little*

Susitna River (57 miles/92 km. long), a favorite with the region's fishermen, is well-known for its king salmon run (late May and June) and one of the largest silver salmon runs (July and August) in all of Southcentral Alaska. *Houston,* on the other side of the river, was homesteaded in the 1950s and is now a popular stopping place for fishermen headed for some portion of the Little Susitna.

Twelve miles (19 km.) from the river on the George Parks is the village of *Willow,* a little piece of Florida swampland just south of 62° North latitude. Actually, in 1976, Willow was chosen by the state legislature to be the site of the new state capital after it was decided that Juneau, the existing capital, was too remote from the rest of the state, as well as the Lower 48. Human nature being what it is, word of the decision sparked a minor real estate boom in Willow. Six years later, however, the state's voters refused to fund the project, and Willow's boom went bust. Given the somewhat precarious state of the Alaskan economy, it's doubtful that Willow will be roused from its slumber any time in the near future.

Talkeetna (112 miles/182 km. from Anchorage, including the distance traveled on the spur road), which is located at the end of a 15-mile- (23- km.-) long spur road off the George Parks, is a typical Alaskan bush community with much of the rough-hewn

charm of its pioneering days still intact. From the banks of the broad and sluggish Susitna River you can get your first look at mighty Mount McKinley—providing the often fickle weather cooperates (remember: the Alaska Range is a weather-maker par excellence). The town, whose only paved road is its frontier-style Main Street, is a favorite departure point for climbing parties with their sights fixed on McKinley's massive bulk. At times in late spring, the babel of foreign languages and climbing argot overheard at the Fairview Inn or Talkeetna Roadhouse can cause you to think you have taken a wrong turn and somehow ended up in Katmandu. The climbers are transported to their base camps on the glaciers at the foot of the mountain by any of the half dozen or so bush pilots (including Lowell Thomas, Jr.) who operate air charter services out of Talkeetna. These same pilots will be happy to take non-climbing visitors on breathtaking flightseeing tours of McKinley and its neighbors.

In addition to its role as a base for the climbing activities that go on in Denali every spring and summer, Talkeetna is well known among fishermen for the summer runs of king and silver salmon that make their way up the Susitna and its tributaries to spawn. The town is also headquarters for a number of float trip and fishing charter outfits.

Finally, every second Saturday in July since the early 1970s, Talkeetna celebrates its *Moose Dropping Festival,* complete with an air show and a colorful parade in which many of the locals participate bedecked in the buckskins and furs of a bygone era. Undoubtedly the highlight of the festivities is the riotous Moose Dropping Throwing Contest, in which contestants stand in a large circle and toss gold spray-painted moose droppings into the center (the sourdough version of pitching pennies); the person who lands one closest to the center wins a cash prize. The money raised at the various stalls and sideshows (including the Moose Dropping Throwing Contest) goes to the *Talkeetna Museum,* an old schoolhouse that has been converted into a museum devoted to the history of the town and surrounding area.

After you've visited Talkeetna, backtrack down the spur road to the George Parks and head north. The highway now runs along the southeastern flank of the Alaska Range in the valley of the *Chulitna River,* a brown and turbulent glacier stream, with fantastic glimpses of the snow-covered peaks of the highest range of mountains in North America urging you on your way.

After providing a spectacular show (in good weather), the George Parks finally cuts through the Alaska Range at *Broad Pass* (2,300 feet/701 meters), the divide between the Cook Inlet and Yukon River watersheds. Although the summit of the pass

(231 miles/372 km. from Anchorage, including the round-trip mileage on the Talkeetna spur road) is one of the lowest in the western half of North America, you're likely to feel as if you're standing on top of the world. This wide mountain valley, surrounded by towering peaks, is only able to support a scanty growth of scrub spruce, a reflection of the fact that it's almost at timberline, as well as the fact that it's frequently scoured by strong winds (something to keep in mind if you're towing a trailer). The Indians and early settlers of the area know it as Caribou Pass, due to the large numbers of these animals that have used it for centuries to escape the bitter winters of the Interior north of the Alaska Range.

On the other side of Broad Pass, you'll soon enter the deep canyon of the *Nenana River,* which has its headwaters in the surrounding mountains and flows northward into the Tanana River, one of the major tributaries of the mighty Yukon. At the 266-mile (428-km.) mark from Anchorage, the entrance to Alaska's most beautiful and accessible national park will come up on your left.

***Denali National Park and Preserve

Denali, the "High One," was the name given North America's tallest peak (20,320 feet/6,195 meters) by the Athapaskan Indians, the region's original inhabitants. The huge massif got its present name in 1897 when William Dickey, an ardent advocate of the gold standard and an amateur prospector who had spent the summer camping south of the mountain, returned to the Lower 48 and wrote an article about his recent adventures. He proposed that Alaska's highest mountain be named after Senator William McKinley, who was running for President and supported Dickey's beloved gold standard. Of course, McKinley went on to win the presidency, the name caught on, and, in 1917, the federal government designated the mountain and 3,000 square miles (8,000 square km.) around it as Mount McKinley National Park. Sixty-three years later, in 1980, the size of the park was more than tripled, to 9,250 square miles (24,000 square km.), and its name was changed to Denali National Park and Preserve, although the showpiece retained the name of McKinley. Almost ten years later, despite a lot of local support in favor of a return to the old Indian name, Mount McKinley it remains.

The mountain itself rises in solitary grandeur out of the 600-mile- (1,000-km.-) long arc of the Alaska Range, a young mountain range that is still in the process of being tectonically uplifted. The dazzlingly white bulk of McKinley looms more than 18,000 feet (5,500 meters) above the surrounding foothills—a rise in elevation from base to peak that is greater than that of any mountain *in the world,* including Mount Everest. Given its great elevation and the fact it's situated north of 62° North latitude, the entire massif is heavily glaciated; at its higher elevations, some of the world's most extreme weather prevails. Even in summer, storms with winds of over 95 miles (150 km.) an hour can whip the snow up into raging blizzards and send temperatures at the summit plummeting to −40°F (−40°C).

The lower elevations of the park also reflect the severity of the climate on and around McKinley and its towering neighbors. Here, at first glance, the elements and their ally, permafrost, seem to have conspired to exclude all but the most tenacious forms of plant and animal life. For as far as the eye can see, the rolling foothills are carpeted by greenish-brown tundra and, occasionally, the darker green of the taiga (sub-Arctic coniferous forest). But a closer inspection (preferably with a park naturalist nearby to answer your questions) will reveal that the tundra in Denali is an incredibly complex and fragile ecosystem, with over 430 species of wildflowers, mosses, lichens, and trees coexisting happily against all odds. This varied and abundant plant life is, in turn, able to support an elaborate food chain that includes, at the top, the largest predators in North America. It won't be long, once you're inside the boundaries of the park, before you begin to notice the parade: voles, squirrels, snow shoe hares, red fox, lynx,

Dall sheep, caribou, wolves, moose, and grizzly bear; ravens, horned owls, and ptarmigans; and, in the park's rivers and streams, trout and grayling. In fact, these days most of the half million visitors to the park in a given year come as much to see Denali's abundant wildlife as they do to gaze upon the awe-inspiring bulk of Mount McKinley.

And then there are those who feel compelled to scale that bulk. The serious exploration of these mountains only began a hundred years ago. In 1910, four gold prospectors from Fairbanks climbed Mount McKinley on a bet, despite the fact that they had absolutely no experience climbing mountains. True to their rugged sourdough heritage, two of the men—Billy Taylor and Pete Anderson—did manage to reach the summit—except that it was the summit visible from Fairbanks, called North Peak today, which is some 850 feet (260 meters) lower than South Peak. As a result, the men (who were scorned as fabulists until a second expedition found the spruce pole they claimed to have left at the summit of North Peak) were denied their "first." That honor went, instead, to Walter Harper, a young Athapaskan Indian from the nearby village of Nenana, who reached the summit of South Peak in 1913.

Nowadays, several hundred climbers manage the ascent every year. Although the climb isn't particularly difficult, technically speaking, running as it does over the glaciers that blanket McKinley from top to bottom, the unpredictable and oftentimes extreme weather does claim its victims, such as the three British climbers who perished there in the early spring of 1989.

The only accommodations available within the park itself are those you'll find at the seven campgrounds spaced out along its solitary road (a total of 225 sites, allocated on a first-come, first-serve basis—which means they're usually gone by 11:00 A.M. during the busy summer season); at its one hotel (the Denali National Park Hotel, located near the railroad station at the entrance to the park); and at three wilderness lodges located 90 miles (144 km.) west of the park entrance at the end of the park road. Outside the boundaries of the park you'll find a range of accommodations, from deluxe lodges to rustic cabins, all of them located along the George Parks Highway. For more information, see the "Practical Information" section at the back of this guide.

The only road in Denali National Park runs along the northern slope of the Alaska Range for a distance of 90 miles (144 km.), and offers, for all but the most uncompromising purist, the easiest access into the unspoiled tundra landscapes of the park's interior. In the not-too-distant past it was possible to drive the length of this road in your own vehicle, but the completion of the George Parks Highway in 1972 greatly increased traffic in the park, and private vehicles were soon restricted to the first 18 miles (29 km.) in order to reduce their impact on Denali's wildlife. To assist people beyond this point, a shuttle bus system was created to take visitors into and out of the park on a daily, regularly scheduled basis (summer only).

Today, the Denali shuttle bus system is a model of responsible, environmentally aware planning, and the wildlife in the vicinity of the park road has rebounded to pre-1972 levels—a happy consequence for animals and animal-lovers alike. You can get maps of the park, shuttle bus timetables and tickets, and tips on looking after yourself in the wilderness at the *Riley Creek Information Center* at the park entrance. (If you're planning on spending a night or more in Denali, you must pack your food and fuel in with you: Open campfires are not allowed in this fragile sub-Arctic environment. Your last chance to shop for supplies will be at the little store at the entrance to the park. And remember: whatever you pack in—fuel canisters, food packaging, or any other non-biodegradable product—*must* be packed out.) When planning your itinerary, don't forget that your best chance of seeing Mount McKinley, which creates its own weather and is often shrouded in clouds, will be in the early morning or late afternoon. It's also the best time to take photographs.

The road itself runs through mighty glacier valleys to the *Eielson Visitor Center,* 65 miles (105 km.) from the park entrance, where most of the buses will turn around for the return leg of the seven-hour round trip. Eielson affords what are probably the finest views of the foothills and soaring, glaciated summits of the Alaska Range, but you can ask your bus driver to let you off at any point along the road, head off to explore the flower-spangled tundra on your own, and return to the road to be picked up by a later bus. Apart from a few footpaths at its entrance, there are no trails in the park: any hiking away from the road will be bushwhacking in the true sense of the word. If you do run into what appears to be a trail, chances are it's been made by animals bigger than you—and, sometimes, animals that won't always be happy to share it.

Each day, a few buses go beyond the Eielson Visitor Center to *Wonder Lake,* another 20 miles (32 km.) farther west, and one of the most photogenic spots in all of Denali National Park. Every bend in this stretch of road holds the promise of a magnificent view—be it dusty-green tundra, silt-filled rivers, or unperturbed wildlife. If your visit to the park is going to last more than a day, however, you must register with the park rangers at the Eielson Visitor Center: To avoid putting stress on the fragile environment, only a limited number of campers are allowed into Denali's back country at any given time. (The same holds true for climbers.)

A visit to Denali National Park will be an experience you're likely to remember for a lifetime. Few places in North America remain as unspoiled, and fewer still preserve nature on such a monumental scale. Whether you're stopping for the day or have plans to explore the more remote reaches of the park over the course of a week, Denali will both delight and awe you, haunt and inspire you. If you're like most people who come to see the "High One," the memory of its massive presence will stir you for years to come, always there in the back of your mind to remind you of the power and majesty of nature.

*

From the turnoff for Denali on your left, the George Parks Highway continues northward through the narrow canyon of the Nenana River, one of Alaska's more popular and accessible river rafting destinations. At the 278-mile (446-km.) mark from Anchorage, you'll pass the short spur road to *Healy,* site of the Usibelli Mine, the oldest coal mine in the state. The slag heaps from this huge operation, which produce over a million and a half tons annually, are all too obvious on the east side of the valley, but Healy residents will tell you that's the price they're willing to pay for economic security.

At this point of the trip, you'll also notice that you've left the towering mountains of the Alaska Range behind and entered a broad, open basin. Although you won't see a sign announcing it, you are now entering the Alaskan Interior.

Interior Alaska

The valley of the *Yukon River,* Alaska's longest (and, with its Canadian portion figured in, North America's fourth-longest), runs like some gigantic trough in a broad arc across the state from northeast to southwest. Bounded on the south by the Alaska Range and the north by the Brooks Range, this huge, virtually uninhabited region is braided by rivers and covered by vast expanses of taiga, the sub-Arctic forest of birch, aspen, cottonwood (alongside streams and riverbanks), spruce, and fir. Most of it remains pristine and untrammeled, largely because of the extremes of temperature and daylight that characterize the region. Only the valley of the *Tanana River* and left-bank tributary of the Yukon have been settled to any real extent, and that is only because of the pioneering efforts of thousands of gold-seekers who flocked to the Fairbanks area at the turn of the century.

Nenana (population 540), 334 miles (536 km.) from Anchorage (including the round trip on Talkeetna spur road), is situated at the confluence of the Nenana and Tanana rivers, and was "founded" in 1902 when a sharp character by the name of Jim Duke built a roadhouse and trading post here. It remained little more than a sleepy outpost, however, while the real action was happening north and east in Fairbanks, until the Alaska Railroad came to town, at which point it experienced its own mini-boom as a construction camp.

Today, Nenana is an important transportation center where building materials, fuel, and a shopping list of other goods are transferred from semi-trucks to large barges and then floated down the Tanana and Yukon rivers to the isolated settlements of western Alaska. In dramatic contrast to this bustling commercial activity, at other points along the river you'll see the fish wheels of the region's Athapaskan Indians—ingenious wooden contraptions that are driven by the current and, after the fashion of a dredger, scoop up passing fish and deposit them into the fisherman's boat.

Nenana is best known, however, for its annual *Ice Classic,* a lottery patronized every spring by more than half the people in the state. The object is to predict the exact day, hour, and minute that the ice holding the river hostage will break up; the winner usually collects upwards of $100,000. Since the first Classic in 1918, the earliest the break-up has ever occurred has been April 20, at 3:27 P.M. (1940), and the latest, May 20, at 11:41 A.M. (1964).

From Nenana, the George Parks Highway swings in a north-easterly direction into the valley of the Tanana River, which is soon cradled by the hills of the *Chena Ridge* and affords sweeping views of the northern flank of the Alaska

Range. As you get closer to Fairbanks you'll begin to notice large spoil heaps in valley bottoms left behind by frenetic gold mining operations. A short side road on your left, at the 380-mile (613-km.) mark from the start of your journey, will take you to the little settlement of *Ester* (population 166) and the old *Malamute Saloon*—made famous by the Robert Service ballad "The Shooting of Dan McGrew," and, with candles on its tables and sawdust on the floor, a charming reminder of how turn-of-the-century prospectors celebrated striking it rich.

Fairbanks

Fairbanks (387 miles/623 km. from Anchorage; population 25,000) is the second-largest city in Alaska and the unofficial capital of the Interior. It's also the region's commercial and transportation center, and all roads seem to either end or begin here, including the George Parks Highway; the Richardson Highway (which joins up with the Alaska Highway at Delta Junction to the southeast); the Steese and Elliott highways (which head deeper into the Interior to the northeast and northwest, respectively); and the Dalton Highway, or Pipeline Haul Road (which heads due north over the Brooks Range and down the long North Slope to Prudhoe Bay on the ice-bound shores of the Beaufort Sea). And that's it: every other square mile to the east, west, and north of the "Golden Heart" of the Interior—about two-thirds of the state—is inaccessible by car, truck, or recreational vehicle; if you want to get there, you're going to have to fly or take a boat—and that's the way most Alaskans like it.

The city itself has a short but colorful history. Just after the turn of the century, while gold fever was still raging in the boomtowns of Nome and Dawson City, an enterprising ex-convict by the name of E. T. Barnette decided he could make his fortune by setting up a trading post on the Eagle-to-Valdez trail, especially if it was established where the trail crossed the Tanana River (in the vicinity of present-day Tanacross); that way he could capture the business of prospectors using the trail *or* the river. So, in the summer of 1901, Barnette bought a stern-wheeler, purchased his supplies, and, with his wife Isabelle, set off up the Yukon River from St. Michael on the Bering Sea. Unfortunately, Barnette was a better hustler than he was a navigator, and his stern-wheeler was soon high and dry on the rocks—which is exactly where Barnette's scheme would have been if he hadn't been able to convince the captain of another boat to take him, Isabelle, and the supplies upriver in return for a 50 percent share of the profits.

Barnette's odyssey had just begun, however. His new partner headed the boat up the Yukon and then the Tanana, until their progress was halted at a shallow part of the river known as Bates Rapids.

Barnette was able to talk his partner into turning around and heading up the Chena River, claiming it would rejoin the Tanana. As soon as it became obvious it wouldn't, Barnette's erstwhile partner dumped him, Isabelle, and their supplies on the bank of the river, dissolved the partnership, and steamed away from the fortune that E. T. Barnette—albeit unexpectedly—was about to make.

Before Barnette could despair, two tired prospectors appeared out of nowhere. Felix Pedro and Tom Gilmour had watched the whole scene from a hillside some miles north and figured they might be able to purchase much-needed supplies from the stranded newcomers. Barnette sold them what they needed, the two prospectors disappeared back into the wilderness, and E. T. continued with his scheming. He soon sent for his brother-in-law, who, in time, arrived from Montana to guard the supplies. In the spring of 1903, Barnette and his wife eventually returned to Seattle for additional supplies and a more suitable boat. While they were gone, Felix Pedro returned to the supply site with the news that he'd struck gold, and by the time Barnette and Isabelle returned to the banks of the Chena, Alaska's newest gold rush was on.

Needless to say, Barnette stayed planted where he was, and by the summer of 1904, a frontier boomtown had sprouted up around his knocked-together trading post. Shortly thereafter, E. T. Barnette was voted the town's first mayor. To gain the support of the region's only federal judge, he agreed to name the settlement after a friend of the judge, Senator Charles Fairbanks (who later became vice president under Theodore Roosevelt).

In spite of its inhospitable winters, Fairbanks grew quickly; by 1910 it had a population of 11,000, most of them prospectors or merchants. As was the case elsewhere, however, the restless prospectors moved on as soon as the gold was mined out, and the population of the town dropped dramatically. Fairbanks struggled to hang on; it was given a much-needed boost in the 1920s by the construction of the Alaska Railroad, which secured its future as a supply center for outlying regions and as a gateway to the Far North. The construction of two military installations during the Second World War, Eilson Air Base and Ladd Field (now Fort Wainwright), provided even greater economic security. Fairbanks' future was guaranteed with the completion of the Alaska Highway in 1942, which made the town accessible to automobile traffic for the first time.

Like its big sister to the south, Fairbanks suffered catastrophic damage at the hand of Mother Nature in the 1960s when the Chena River flooded its banks and put most of the town under eight feet (2.5 meters) of water. The disaster was quickly forgotten when it was announced in 1968 that vast oil reserves had been discovered in the Arctic. Seemingly overnight, Fairbanks became the advance base of operations for the oil companies involved in exploring the region. By the time the legal and environmental issues were settled some five years later, it also had been named headquarters for the Alyeska Pipeline Service Company (see page 32), the consortium charged with building the Trans-Alaska Pipeline. For the second time during this century Fairbanks became a boomtown, as well-paid welders and roughnecks flocked north to the edge of the wilderness. At its height, the pipeline boom saw the population of Fairbanks double to some 35,000, its rental rates shoot through the roof, and its frontier-town history repeat itself with a vengeance. Just as the crowds moved on when the gold was tapped out during the early part of this century, so went the throng when the pipeline was completed; thus, the bonanza went bust by the late 1970s. Pipeline workers filled the town for one last time, then headed south, leaving behind a town out of breath, full of memories, and stuck with a sky-high cost of living.

Today, Fairbanks is a bit smaller than it was during its pipeline heyday, a lot more sedate, and, all things considered, a nicer place to visit—especially during its surprisingly warm summers (it regularly records the highest summertime temperatures in the state). Summer is also its busiest season, with everybody from wilderness campers to elderly motorists seeming to converge on the place. If your itinerary includes Fairbanks at this time of year, be sure to make reservations in advance and don't be surprised if the rates seem high—they will be. If you're the type who can do without a roof overhead for a day or two, there are a number of places to camp within the city limits, and even more within an hour's drive on any of the major highways leading into or out of town. (For a complete list, contact the State Division of Parks; see the "Practical Information" section at the back of this guide for the address.)

In many respects, Fairbanks is a typical modern American city, complete with malls, subdivisions, and its fair share of urban tackiness. The downtown area is clustered around a bend of the meandering Chena River, with its numbered avenues running east to west parallel to the river, and its major streets running perpendicular to them in a north-south direction. The **Fairbanks Visitor Information Center,** probably the best place to start your tour of the city, is located at First Avenue and Cushman Street, near the spot where E.T. Barnette was abandoned by an irate steamboat captain some 90 years ago. Directly across the river and the Cushman Street Bridge is the *Immaculate Conception Church*, the oldest church in Fairbanks (c. 1904). It was moved to its present location on rollers from the south side of the river in 1911 after the Chena froze over for the winter.

For those interested in a slightly gimmicky look at what frontier life in Fairbanks was like, **Alaskaland,** at Peger Road and Airport Way, is a 44-acre open-air museum complete with its own narrow-gauge railroad, an old stern-wheeler, a re-created native village, a well-restored gold rush town, a couple of museums, and much more. A bus disguised as a train picks up visitors at the city's hotels throughout the day for those who'd like to leave their cars behind.

Another favorite with summertime visitors is a trip down the Chena and Tanana rivers on one of the two authentic stern-wheelers, the *Discovery* and *Discovery II,* operated by Jim and Mary Binkley. The Binkley family has been doing much the same thing for four generations, first for miners and now for tourists, and Captain Jim himself probably knows the Tanana and its tributaries better than anyone alive today.

The **University of Alaska-Fairbanks,** situated on a hill across the Chena and west of downtown, is the oldest and largest institution of higher learning in the state. Established in 1917 as the Alaska Agricultural College and School of Mines, UAF today is known worldwide for the quality and comprehensiveness of its Arctic studies programs. The campus itself is a self-sufficient community, with its own television station, radio station, post office, fire station, and network of underground passages to facilitate getting around during the long, bitterly cold winters. Summertime visitors to Fairbanks can avail themselves of a variety of activities and things to see on the UAF campus, including the *Fairbanks Research Farm* (more of those oversized Alaskan vegetables), geophysical and mineral research labs that are open to the public on certain days of the week, the *Large Animal Research Station* (musk ox, caribou, reindeer, and moose), and a student union that offers inexpensive lunches and dinners Monday through Friday.

The *Otto William Geist Museum* on campus is a must for anyone interested in the native peoples or natural history of Alaska. Its excellent collection is divided among five sections— each devoted, in turn, to one of the state's major geographical regions—illustrating everything from patterns of human settlement to the impact of oil production on the Arctic environment. And for anyone who doubts that Alaska is a land of large—sometimes very large—mammals, the 10-foot- (3-meter-) high Kodiak bear guarding the entrance serves as a reminder of what you can find in the Great Land. (Don't worry— the bear is stuffed.) Guided tours of the museum are offered Monday through Friday (call 907-474-NEWS for more information).

Side trips from Fairbanks. There are a variety of side trips you can take by car from Fairbanks, any one of which will give you a good idea of the vastness of the Alaskan Interior.

Probably the most popular with Fairbanks residents and visitors from the Lower 48 alike, is the 60-mile (100-km.) jaunt along the upper course of the Chena River to **Chena Hot Springs.** If nothing else, the drive itself is reason enough to make the trip. Turning right off the Steese Highway onto *Chena Hot Springs Road*, you'll soon leave the suburbs and farmland surrounding Fairbanks behind and find yourself amidst the dense forests of the *Chena Valley.* Beaver dams will be a common sight on either side of the road, and lumbering moose will be encountered almost as frequently as a car heading in the opposite direction. The sulfur springs at the end of the road have attracted sore and tired miners since their discovery in 1907. Today the waters are piped into a handsome indoor swimming pool attached to an equally attractive lodge (both are open year-round). In summer, there are miles of trails leading into the surrounding wilderness, and hiking, fishing, badminton, and volleyball are just some of the activities enjoyed by guests. During the winter, the trails fill with cross-country skiers (rentals available at the lodge) who quickly learn that there are few pleasures in life greater than sliding into a hot mineral water bath after a long day of strenuous exercise.

For the more adventurous, the Steese Highway heads north out of Fairbanks and then swings to the northeast, pushing 162 miles (260 km.) into the wilderness before it reaches its terminus at *Circle* on the Yukon River. Only the first 71 km. (44 miles) of the Steese are paved, however, which includes the mileage to the old mining communities of Fox and Chatanika. After that, it's a wide, well-maintained gravel road affording great views of the White Mountains and the Chatanika River. Eventually, it reaches *Central* (128 miles/206 km. from Fairbanks), another tiny community dating back to the gold rush days at the turn of the century, where it narrows considerably for the last 34 miles (55 km.) into Circle, on the Yukon River. Central is also where you pick up the spur road to **Circle Hot Springs,** a little oasis in the heart of rugged gold mining country only 8 miles (13 km.) from the turnoff. First discovered in 1893, the hot mineral springs were homesteaded a year or so after Felix Pedro struck gold north of Fairbanks. Today, the lodge in town is open year-round and offers rooms, cabins, a saloon, dining facilities, and an Olympic-sized swimming pool.

At the end of the Steese Highway sits quiet little **Circle** (population 94), which is only 50 miles (80 km.) south of the Arctic Circle (it was given its name by the first miners to settle here, who thought it *was* on the Arctic Circle), and is one of the northernmost points in the United States accessible by car. Even when the "summer people" return in late May, swelling its population to almost 800, it's hard to imagine that this was, in the days before the Klondike Gold Rush, the largest town on the Yukon River. Nowadays, the Yukon still figures prominently in the town's life, and the waterfront bustles with activity in the summer as the river fills with freight barges, boats, and canoes. Located midway between the boundaries of the Yukon Flats National Wildlife Refuge and the Yukon-Charley National Preserve, Circle is a popular stop with float-trippers on their way down the river. For true adventurers willing to brave the area in the dead of winter, the Steese Highway is maintained year-round (except for Mondays and Tuesdays when it is not patrolled—try not to travel on these days, as you may find yourself stranded). You won't need reservations at the hot springs during the winter—which is the reason why many people are tempted to make the trip at this time. Before you succumb to temptation, just remember: temperatures can drop as low as $-70°F$ ($-56°C$) in this part of Alaska, and you'd be foolhardy not to take precautions if you decide to make the trip: bring along a warm sleeping bag; extra food, water, and clothing; a heat source; and, to be doubly safe, notify a friend or relative before you head out.

There's still another mineral hot springs within a day's drive of Fairbanks: **Manley Hot Springs,** at the end of the *Elliott Highway,* is almost as far north and west of Fairbanks—152 miles (245 km.)—as Circle is northeast. The Elliott branches off from the Steese Highway at *Fox,* 11 miles (18 km.) north of Fairbanks, and is paved for its first 28 miles (45 km.). Hard-packed gravel covers the remaining 124 miles (200 km.), and the road is generally in good condition, although it narrows and becomes trickier to drive as you near Manley. (Heavy rain can also cause it to become treacherous.) Views of the White Mountains alternate with those of densely forested valleys. Like the Steese, the Elliott Highway is open year-round, but drivers who plan to tackle it during the winter should do so with a healthy dose of respect and survival gear. For road conditions, check with the Alaska Department of Transportation in Fairbanks.

Just past *Livengood* (73 miles/118 km. from Fairbanks), a small community of a hundred people that got its start—as so many in the area did—as a mining settlement, the *Pipeline Haul Road* (see page 13) begins its roller coaster ride north to Prudhoe Bay. Before it reaches Manley, the Elliott Highway continues to the left and passes only one other community, *Minto* (110 miles/177 km. from Fairbanks). This Athapaskan Indian village of some 200 people was relocated here in 1971 after the Tanana River flooded its original site.

Aside from its distinction as the home of two-time Iditarod winner Susan Butcher, *Manley* is best known for its hot springs, which have no sulfur content—and thus no "eggy" smell—as well as for having one of the friendliest roadhouses in the state (especially at race time). With Ms. Butcher and other sled dog enthusiasts in residence, dog lovers visiting the area stand a good chance of bumping into someone who just might know a thing or two about training dogs.

*

From Fairbanks, the Alaska Highway picks up the *Richardson Highway*—Alaska's oldest road. Its history dates back to the gold rush era, when it was part of the Eagle-to-Valdez trail. It heads through the valley of the Tanana River, which is quite wide and dotted with sandbars at this point. From the low hills on either side of the river are grand views over the ramified glacier valley to the summits of the Alaska Range, including *Mount Hayes* (13,832 feet/4,216 meters). You may feel the urge to pinch yourself to make sure you're not dreaming when you come to *North Pole,* about 14 miles (22 km.) southeast of Fairbanks. Besides being a bedroom community of Alaska's second-largest city, North Pole is also the home of *Santa Claus House,* the brainchild of a local entrepreneur. As you may have guessed, it is well known to children all over the country as the home of Mr. Claus. By unofficial count, half the people in this community of 1,000 are kept busy answering Santa's mail during the holiday season.

Delta Junction, 485 miles (780 km.) from Anchorage (including the round trip on the Talkeetna spur road), is a typical Alaskan supply center that stretches for some 8 miles (13 km.) on either side of the highway. Founded as a construction camp for the Richardson Highway in 1919, it became known as Buffalo Center after a herd of American bison was transplanted here in the 1920s. More recently, and in spite of the often extreme climate, the community has become the center of the state's efforts to develop an agricultural industry in the region based on barley. The state set up an auction to determine qualified buyers of land it had set aside for agricultural development; then, those who were eligible participated in a lottery to choose and purchase the land. Since 1978, over 70,000 acres have been disposed of by the state, most of it flat ground north of town. Over a third of the land has been successfully brought under cultivation, with harvests yielding barley and oats, among other crops.

Delta Junction is also the official end of the Alaska Highway, which becomes the *Richardson Highway* at the famous "last milestone" next to the Visitor Center. Another much photographed local sight is the *Trans-Alaska Pipeline,* which crosses the Tanana River in a glistening arch just west of town. The pipeline parallels the Richardson Highway as it heads due south over the Alaska Range to *Glennallen* (151 miles/243 km.

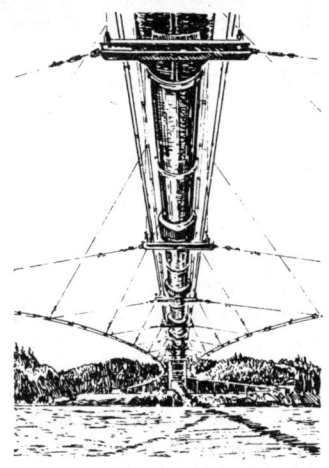

The Trans-Alaska Pipeline
at Delta Junction

from Delta Junction) and, eventually, *Valdez* on Prince William Sound. This is a magnificently scenic road that takes you past spectacular glaciers, spruce forests, and sub-Arctic tundra. One of its highlights is *Isabel Pass* (3,000 feet/914 meters), but there are many others to distract you along the route.

If you have the time, however, we recommend that you stay on the Alaska Highway as it continues in a southeasterly direction. Along the way, you'll cross one broad, glacier-fed tributary

THE ALASKA
HWY NO 1

stream after another, all of them flanked by deposits of gravel as they hurry on their way to the Tanana River.

Tok (593 miles/954 km. from Anchorage) got its start as a construction camp during the building of the Alaska Highway in 1942, and was originally called "Tokyo Camp." Later, to get rid of its association with Japan, the name of the settlement and nearby river was shortened to its present version (it rhymes with *poke*). Situated at the junction of two of the state's most important roads, the Alaska Highway and the Tok Cut-Off to the Glenn Highway (which ends in Anchorage), Tok is the gateway to Alaska for overland travelers coming from the east. (It's a day's drive from here to either Fairbanks or Anchorage.) The *Visitor Center,* located at the junction to these two highways, has an interesting exhibit of Alaskan fauna. The town is also famed throughout the North as the "Sled Dog Capital of Alaska." The winter racing season, which begins in November, is a long and busy one, but summertime visitors can also get a look at these wonderful animals in action at the 12.5-mile- (20-km.-) long training track that runs alongside the Alaska Highway.

Side trip to Canada

The legendary Canadian gold rush town of **Dawson City** (182 miles/293 km. from Tok) makes for a fascinating two-day side trip

from Tok. The route, which follows the Taylor Highway (becoming Highway 9 on the other side of the Canadian border), provides a beautiful drive along the "top of the world" into rugged gold mining country. It is only open in summer, however, and even then, it is a narrow, twisting gravel road with steep hills and occasional soft spots. Motorists should allow for unforseen delays, and those in large recreational vehicles or pulling a trailer should use extra caution when making this trip.

After the discovery of gold in nearby *Bonanza Creek* in 1896, a trader named Joe Ladue staked out the site of a town on the level ground at the mouth of the Klondike River; thus, Dawson City was born. Within a short time, a motley assemblage of saloons, stores, hotels, restaurants, and even theaters had been built; boardwalks ran the length of the streets so that pedestrians might avoid the knee-deep mud that made them virtually impassable in spring.

After the first great finds, a lucky few were able to treat themselves to every conceivable luxury. The finest porcelain graced their tables, mirrors from Paris embellished the gambling dens they frequented, and Scotch whiskey enlivened their evenings—all brought in steamers across the Bering Strait and then 1,240 miles (2,000 km.) up the Yukon River. By 1900, when it had a population of 30,000 (making it the biggest town in western Canada), Dawson City was known as the "Paris of the North."

After the gold rush petered out, the town settled down into a long decline. Since the mid 1970s, it has enjoyed a bit of a revival: higher prices for gold have attracted new gold-seekers, plus the Canadian government has restored some of the town's historic buildings. Today, Dawson City is a lively, colorful place, the pride of the locals and a great tourist attraction.

You can see all the most interesting sights in town by just walking down the creaking boardwalks. The best starting point is the *Visitor Reception Center* (King and Front Streets), where you can get maps and information, see an audiovisual show, and join a conducted tour.

Diagonally opposite, on the banks of the Yukon, is the *SS Keno*, a beautifully restored sternwheeler. Next to it is the *Bank of Commerce*, considered one of the most important buildings in town—at least by the prospectors of bygone days. The poet Robert Service was a clerk here for some years, and in the *Gold Room* you can see a small exhibit of assay equipment.

On King Street, one block beyond the visitor center, is the reconstructed Wild West façade of the *Palace Grand Theatre*, built by "Arizona Charlie" Meadows in 1899. On summer evenings you can watch a production of the *Gaslight Follies*, a typical turn-of-the-century revue.

Opposite the theater is the *Old Post Office*, where customers are still served much as they were in

Palace Grand Theatre, Dawson City

1901. Letters mailed from here are postmarked by hand.

Diamond Tooth Gertie's Gambling Hall (Queen Street and 4th Avenue), which has also been restored in the style of the period, is Canada's only legal gambling casino.

The *Dawson City Museum* (Church Street and 5th Avenue) has the country's largest collection of gold-rush memorabilia—maps, tools, historic photographs, and old locomotives used on the mining railroad. You can also see fascinating silent films here of life in Dawson City in the 20th century.

Robert Service's Cabin, behind the museum on 8th Avenue, is the log cabin that the "Bard of the Yukon" *(Songs of a Sourdough, Ballads of a Cheechako)* built for himself. Scottish-born Service came to Dawson City as a bank clerk and grew to love the Yukon. His poems and ballads capture the

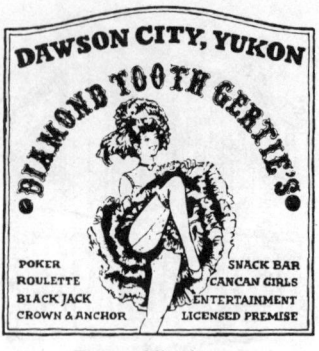

The gambling house

essence of the wild and lonely landscape of the North, as well as the lives of the people who lived there. During the summer there are daily recitals of his works.

A few paces farther on is a reconstruction of *Jack London's Cabin,* where the famous novelist and short-story writer lived for some years. His best-known works (*Call of the Wild* and *White Fang*), like Service's, depict the adventurous life in the North. There are also daily readings from his works during the summer.

The path to the banks of the Yukon will take you through a part of town dotted with abandoned and dilapidated turn-of-the-century structures. A number of handsomely restored buildings such as the *Court House* and the *Commissioner's Residence* on Front Street will give you some idea of the wealth and elegance that characterized the town during the heady gold rush era. In addition, *Harrington's Store,* on 3rd Avenue, has a nice collection of old photographs that captures the "feel" of Dawson City's short-lived but glorious heyday.

One and one-half miles (2 km.) out of town, **Bonanza Creek,** where it all began, flows into the Klondike. The gravel road leading up the valley is flanked here by gigantic mounds of spoil created by the old gold mines as well as by more modern methods, which include dredges and hydraulic apparatus. At *Claim 33,* visitors can try their luck at panning for gold; if you do try, you'll quickly realize what it was like to be a gold-miner: stuck with a perpetually sore back and not much to show for it.

Seven and one-half miles (12 km.) from town, ***Dredge No. 4,** once one of the largest floating gold-panning installations ever constructed, now sits abandoned in the valley. This contraption consisted of a barge with an endless chain of 75 steel buckets, each weighing 2 tons, that dug the gold-

Panning for gold

Dense forest and white mountain peaks form a majestic backdrop to Sitka's harbor.

Indians in ritual dress celebrate a festival in the streets of Alaska's state capital.

Alaska's many waterways offer serenity and seclusion.

At Valdez, the Richardson Highway cuts through the heavily glaciated Chugach Mountains.

The traditional Eskimo blanket toss, once used for whale sightings, is now a rollicking event at festivals.

Totem poles remain part of the art and culture of Alaska's Native population.

Mountains of ice create dramatic effects in Kenai Fjords.

There is no better place to view America's wildlife than in the huge state and national parks of Alaska.

Buses bring visitors to the Eielson Visitor Center in Denali National Park.

Creek Street in Ketchikan is actually a boardwalk. In summer, salmon can be seen leaping out of the water that flows beneath it.

Grassy slopes and rushing water characterize many vistas in the Southeast.

bearing gravel from the river bottom and unloaded it on the barge. From there, it was washed and then, after the removal of any gold, discharged at the other end. The dredge, which was driven by its own engine, could process 17,000 cubic yards (13,000 cubic meters) of gravel every 24 hours.

Discovery Claim, 1.5 miles (2 km.) above Dredge No. 4, was the spot where George Carmack and his partners found the first nuggets of gold. A tablet now commemorates that day in August 1896 that sparked off the greatest gold rush in history, which eventually led to the recovery of at least $500 million worth of the precious metal.

Before leaving Dawson City you should drive the 5 miles (8 km.) to *Midnight Dome* for the sake of the splendid views, which extend over the town and river to the great mounds of spoil and the *Ogilvie Mountains* in the distance.

*

From Tok, the Tok Cut-Off heads to the southwest and, eventually, Anchorage. Cutting through the Alaska Range at *Mentasta Pass* (2,434 feet/740 meters), the highway leaves behind the Tanana River watershed (part of the larger Yukon River system, which drains into the Bering Sea) and enters the valley of the *Copper River* (which empties into the Gulf of Alaska), an area famed for its abundance of wildlife. To the south are the snow-covered summits of **Wrangell-St. Elias National Park** (13,900 sq. miles/36,000 sq. km.), the largest national park in the United States. Along with adjoining *Kluane National Park* in the Yukon Territory, Wrangell-St. Elias has been designated a World Heritage Site by UNESCO.

Dominated by the two mighty mountain ranges for which it is named, the volcanic *Wrangell Mountains* and the sedimentary and volcanic *St. Elias Mountains,* this wild and completely undeveloped park contains the largest concentration of peaks exceeding 14,100 feet (4,300 meters) in North America. It also boasts nine of the sixteen highest peaks in the United States, two of which—*Mount Sanford* (16,238 feet/4,950 meters) and *Mount Wrangell* (14,163 feet/4,317 meters)—command the horizon as you travel southwest toward Glennallen along with the smaller *Mount Drum* (12,010 feet/3,660 meters). Far to the south, *Mount St. Elias* (18,008 feet/5,490 meters), Alaska's second-highest peak, and Canada's *Mount Logan* (19,850 feet/6,050 meters), across the border in Kluane National Park and North America's second tallest mountain, soar above the isolated and uninhabited southeastern corner of the state. Because of their precipitous elevations and the large amounts of snow that fall on them, these mountains are heavily glaciated; for instance, the *Malaspina Glacier,* which spills down the southern flank of Mount St. Elias, is the largest piedmont glacier in North America, with an area of some 1,500 square miles (3,885 sq. km.). The adjacent *Hubbard Glacier* is one of the most active glaciers on the continent, and in 1986 actually advanced far enough to seal off Russel Fjord, an extension of Yakutat Bay. Another indication of the geologic youthfulness of these mountains are the numerous earthquakes that strike the region, evidence of the tectonic activity that is still occurring far beneath the earth's surface in this part of the world. Not surprisingly, the entire region is of great interest to volcanologists, glaciologists, and other scientists; it always seems to be hosting a major scientific expedition.

For the wilderness enthusiast, Wrangell-St. Elias National Park embraces landscapes of unparalleled grandeur. The hunting, mountaineering, backpacking, kayaking, and opportunities for wildlife photography in the park are unsurpassed, and compared to its older sister, Denali National Park, it is almost empty during the peak summer season. Access is not a problem: from the north, the park can be reached via the Tok Cut-Off and a gravel spur road that branches off from the highway at *Slana;* and from the south and west, the Richardson Highway connects with the Edgerton Highway, which leads to the old copper mining community of *McCarthy.* For those who plan to spend more than a day in the park, however,

the Park Service warns that you should be self-sufficient and possess wilderness survival skills. Rain gear and warm clothing are essential, and it's always a good idea to leave an itinerary behind with a friend or park ranger. For more information, see the "Practical Information" section at the back of this guide.

Shortly before you come to the busy town of *Glennallen* (731 miles/1,176 km. from the start of Travel Route 1), a popular gateway to the Wrangell Mountains, the Tok Cut-Off joins the Richardson Highway for a distance of 14 miles (23 km.) before it becomes the Glenn Highway and heads off to the west and Anchorage (189 miles/304 km. from the southern junction of the two roads). The Richardson Highway, in the meantime, continues in a southerly direction, following the course of the broad Copper River as it makes its way to Valdez on Prince William Sound. The summits of Mount Drum and Mount Wrangell, Alaska's largest active volcano, dominate the views to the east for much of this stretch, while the otherworldly sight of the pipeline, which parallels the highway for the remaining distance into Valdez, comes into view to the west. Thirty-two miles (52 km.) south of the junction between the Glenn and Richardson highways, the Edgerton Highway (see above) heads off to the east and the historic mining town of McCarthy. (The Edgerton is only paved for its first 35 miles/57 km., as far as the tiny community of *Chitina*. The unpaved McCarthy Road, which begins on the east bank of the Copper River, runs the remaining 58 miles/94 km. through pristine wilderness to McCarthy. The road is narrow and often in less-than-good repair; it is not recommended for large recreational vehicles or cars pulling trailers.)

The Richardson crosses a number of streams, including the Little Tonsina and Tiekel rivers, before it begins its ascent into the Chugach Mountains. Just before the summit of *Thompson Pass* (2,770 feet/845 meters), site of the heaviest snowfalls ever recorded in Alaska (see page 20), the twin tongues of the *Worthington Glacier* extend down almost to the road. The glacier, which heads on Girls Mountain (6,135 feet/1,870 meters) and is the most visited site in the Copper River basin, is accessible via a short road to the left, at the end of which you'll find parking, interpretative displays, and picnic sites. As elsewhere in the Chugach Mountains, the heavy glaciation in this area is due to the tremendous amounts of snow that fall on the surrounding mountains. (Glaciers form when more snow falls over the course of years than melts; the weight of the new snow compresses the old snow underneath it, until, eventually, the compressed older layers of snow are extruded like plastic, "flowing" downhill according to the dictates of gravity.)

On the other side of Thompson Pass the road runs through steep-sided *Keystone Canyon*, which is flanked by foaming waterfalls, before it finally ends at ***Valdez** (839 miles/1,351 km. from the start of Travel Route 1), on the *Valdez Arm* of Prince William Sound.

First established in 1897–1898 as a port of entry for the thousands of gold-seekers scrambling to make their way north to Dawson City, Valdez (population 3,300) has seen more than its fair share of event-filled history. In its early years, the trail into the Interior ran over the hazardous Valdez Glacier, where many lives were lost to crevasses and extreme weather. In the early 1900s, the trail was rerouted through Thompson Pass and widened into a wagon road; that road was extended to Fairbanks and renamed the Richardson Highway in the 1920s.

Until recently, the greatest calamity to hit Valdez was the 1964 Good Friday Earthquake. The tidal wave that it created virtually wiped out the entire town. However, rather than packing it in and moving on, the town's residents, most of them fishermen or people dependent on the commercial fishing industry, decided to relocate and rebuild their town on a new site 4.5 miles (7 km.) to the west. Their perseverance was rewarded in the late 1960s when it was announced that the town's ice-free port (the northernmost in the Western Hemisphere) and link to the Alaska highway system made it the leading candidate to become the southern terminus of the proposed Trans-Alaska Pipeline. And, indeed, in 1977, after the dust arising from legal, political, and environmental questions had settled and construction was completed, Valdezians could look across their sparkling bay to the state-of-the-art *Marine Terminal*, where oil from the North Slope would soon be gravity-fed into huge tanks and supertankers. The seemingly impossible task of reconciling the majestic scenery and prolific fisheries of Prince William Sound with the harsh realities of modern oil production had been pulled off, and almost everyone was happy—from the oil companies to U.S. consumers to the residents of Valdez, who had benefitted from the construction boom and could still enjoy their beloved mountains and Prince William Sound in a virtually pristine state.

Tragically, the impossible proved to be just that in March of 1989, when the supertanker *Exxon Valdez* ran aground on Bligh Reef, a well-known hazard east of the shipping lanes. The resulting spill of 10 million gallons, the largest oil spill in U.S. history, quickly spread over a large area of Prince William Sound, fouled over 800 miles (1,280 km.) of shoreline, and threatened serious damage to the incredibly rich ecosystem that had existed before the disaster.

Although it is too early, as we write, to predict the ultimate extent of the damage, it already has become apparent that the area's marine life and commercial fishermen will be hardest hit. Some experts are predicting that certain fisheries will be adversely affected for five years or more; at the same time, thousands of dead marine mammals and birds have washed up on shore, and the tally is expected to climb much higher. Quite possibly, a third victim could well be the oil companies themselves, as the future of further oil exploration and drilling in Alaska is questioned in light of the *Exxon Valdez* spill. Environmentalists, who were already prepared for a no-holds-barred fight on drilling in the Arctic National Wildlife Refuge, are certain to point to the tragedy and its long-term consequences as proof that oil and wilderness don't mix; the oil companies and their supporters will be just as adamant in their insistence that Alaskan oil is vital to the economic security of the United States. Whatever the outcome, however, the name of the *Exxon Valdez* will likely remain synonymous with the hubris of men seduced by the seeming perfectibility of their machines.

If there was a silver lining to the dark cloud of the *Exxon Valdez* spill, it had to be the fact that the ****Columbia Glacier,** the largest and most celebrated tidewater glacier in Prince William Sound, escaped serious damage. Named after Columbia University in New York City, the glacier covers an area of some 425 square miles

(1,100 sq. km.) and boasts a terminus on Columbia Bay over 6 miles (10 km.) in length and 260 feet (80 meters) high. From this impressive façade, huge chunks of ice break off from time to time with a thunderous roar, churning up the plankton-rich waters of the bay and helping to create an environment that attracts salmon, bald eagles, gulls, whales, dolphins, and harbor seals in great numbers (the seals, which frolic on the icebergs that litter the bay, are a particular favorite with cruise-ship passengers). The intense blue light that emanates from the deep crevasses in the glacier is the result of refraction in the highly compacted ice. Also of interest is the prediction that the glacier will recede some 20 miles (32 km.) over the next 20 to 50 years, due to the global warming trend that will melt much of its bulk. It will leave behind a deep fjord and spawn tens of thousands of icebergs as it retreats, posing a threat to shipping into and out of the Port of Valdez.

From Valdez there are two routes back to *Anchorage*—one by water and one by land.

Valdez to Anchorage overland

(*Follow the route marked 1A on the map on pages 54–55.*)

The overland route—the less expensive of the two—involves backtracking to Glennallen on the

A farm in the Matanuska Valley

Richardson Highway and turning west onto the Glenn Highway (Highway 1).

At the head of the *Matanuska Valley* the view extends from a steep-sided hill over the valley to the snow-capped Chugach Mountains and the 28-mile-(45-km.-) long *Matanuska Glacier,* which emerges from the mountains in a 4-mile-(6-km.-) wide wall of ice. Thousands of years ago, this glacier extended more than 95 miles (150 km.) farther west to the vicinity of present-day Anchorage. Today, a winding road runs through the Glacier Park Resort to the tip of the glacier; with a good pair of boots and a degree of caution, a walk on the light blue ice should be no problem.

At the western end of the valley is *Palmer* (see pages 53–55), and from there it is only 43 miles (68 km.) back to *Anchorage* (1,135 miles/1,826 km. round trip from the beginning of Travel Route 1) and the end of the tour. (A more detailed look at Alaska's largest city begins on page 42.)

Valdez to Anchorage via the Alaska Marine Highway System

(*Follow the route marked 1B on the map on pages 54–55.*)

Though longer, this route, which takes advantage of the *Alaska Marine Highway System,* gives you some idea of the vast area and majestic scenery of Prince William Sound. From Valdez, the spectacular seven-hour trip through fjords and past rocky islands provides fine views of the Columbia and other glaciers.

Whittier, the beautifully situated ferry port at the western end of the Sound, was originally created as a Navy port and petroleum supply center during the Second World War. Today, the little town of 300 (fully half of whom live in a single building, the 14-story Begich Building), is connected to the Alaska highway system by a spur line of the Alaska Railroad, which runs under the Chugach Mountains for 12.5 miles (20 km.) to *Portage.* From there, it's another 48 miles (77 km.) northwest on the Seward Highway to *Anchorage* (887 miles/1,428 km. from the beginning of Travel Route 1, not including the distance covered by ferry and rail).

For a more detailed look at Anchorage, see pages 42–50. For more information about the Alaska Marine Highway System, see the "Practical Information" section at the back of the book.

TRAVEL ROUTE 2: The **Kenai Peninsula: Anchorage–Seward–Kenai–Homer (298 miles/480 km.)

See map on pages 54–55.

For this trip from Anchorage south to the Kenai Peninsula and back again, you should allow three or four days. The first highlight of the trip is Portage Glacier and its small lake filled with miniature icebergs. The excursion to Kenai Fjords National Park takes you into one of the most breathtakingly dramatic national parks in the country, where sea otters and seals sport about at the foot of "calving" glaciers. Before continuing on to the beautifully situated little town of Homer, wilderness enthusiasts may want to try a canoe trip (allow one to four days) into the Kenai National Wildlife Refuge. This area offers an extensive system of connected routes centered around the Swanson and Moose rivers. (Canoes and equipment can be rented at the Swanson River Road turnoff from the Sterling Highway; further information and maps are available from the office of the Kenai National Wildlife Refuge, Box 2139, Soldotna, AK 99669.)

For a more detailed look at **Anchorage,** the starting point of the trip, see pages 42–50.

To get started on this route, leave Anchorage on the Seward Highway, which hugs the northern shore of beautiful *Turnagain Arm* all the way to *Portage,* a distance of 48 miles (77 km.). For a closer look at this stretch, see pages 48–49.

At Portage, you can take the short spur of the Alaska Railroad to *Whittier,* the western terminus for Alaska state ferry runs across magnificent Prince William Sound. (The ferry runs from Whittier to Valdez five times a week during the summer; for more information about the Alaska Marine Highway System, see the "Practical Information" section at the back of the book.)

A short spur road also takes you to *Portage Glacier,* the most visited natural attraction in the state (see page 48 for a more detailed description of the glacier).

The **Kenai Peninsula

South of the narrow neck of land separating Portage and Turnagain Arm from Whittier and Prince William Sound, the mountainous Kenai Peninsula extends for more than 125 miles (200 km.) into the Gulf of Alaska, whose relatively warm currents moderate wintertime temperatures but also bring with them heavy rain and snowfalls. (As a result, the great glaciers in its mountains show no sign of retreating.) Every year, tens of thousands of visitors flock to the peninsula to sample its varied scenery, pleasant climate, and abundant wildlife. Four-fifths of the area has been set aside as a wildlife reserve or national parkland.

From Portage, the Seward Highway (Highway 1) climbs into the dense spruce-and-fir forests of the Kenai Mountains. Shortly after *Turnagain Pass* (59 miles/94 km. from Anchorage), where winter snow depths frequently measure 12 feet (4 meters) or more, you'll come to the Johnson Pass north trailhead. It provides access over a fairly level 23-mile-(37-km.-) long trail to spectacular alpine scenery and great fishing.

Farther on, at the *Tern Lake Junction,* the route swings left onto Highway 9 (still called the Seward Highway) and then heads south toward the coast. The road runs past a number of long mountain lakes in which the lush green mountain slopes are mirrored on calm mornings. There's a modern fish hatchery, established some years ago, on *Upper Trail Lake* (95 miles/152 km. from Anchorage) where you can watch as salmon are "milked" and millions of their tiny fry are fed. In August, you can watch the thousands of brilliant red chum salmon that have swum upstream to spawn in the stream opposite the hatchery. The little settlement of *Moose Pass* (population 145) was founded as a construction camp for the Alaska Railroad in the years before First World War. From here to Seward, the road will run parallel to the railroad tracks.

Seward (127 miles/203 km. from Anchorage), situated at the head of *Resurrection Bay* (so-named by Alexander Baranof, who found shelter here from one of the Gulf of Alaska's fierce storms on Easter Sunday in 1791), is a picturesque community of some 2,200 people surrounded by snow-covered mountains. The town itself was established in 1903 by surveyors who had been charged with laying out a viable rail route to the gold-rush boomtown of Fairbanks and appreciated the site's deep-water harbor (it was, of course, named after Secretary of State William H. Seward, the man most responsible for acquiring Alaska for the United States). The railroad was completed in 1923, but its headquarters were moved north to Anchorage that same year, and Seward settled into peaceful obscurity.

Today, Seward's harbor is the mainstay of its economy. In addition to the large salmon-fishing fleet housed here, Seward is a major coal-shipping port (much of which goes to Korea and other "Pacific Rim" countries) and a popular destination for cruise ships. Every August the town also plays host to the *Silver Salmon Derby,* which attracts both professional and sportfishermen from all over the state and promises over $100,000 in prize money. Another popular summertime event is the

Mount Marathon Race, held every Fourth of July; runners begin in Seward and race to the summit of the 3,022-foot (920-meter) mountain above town and back again.

With its beautiful harbor, access to spectacular alpine scenery, and moderate climate, one can see why Seward sometimes bills itself as "Alaska's one-stop vacation spot." Without a doubt, its greatest attraction is nearby **Kenai Fjords National Park*. The park, with an area of 900 square miles (2,320 sq. km.), encompasses much of the coastal mountain range in the southeastern part of the peninsula, as well as a large part of the 300 square miles (780 sq. km.) of the *Harding Icefield*. Situated high (almost a mile/1.5 km.) above the Gulf of Alaska, the Harding Icefield, like all ice fields, is an area whose phenomenal snowfalls have created glaciers so massive that they cover everything except for the tops, or *nunataks,* of the surrounding mountains (this particular ice field receives between 700–1,000 inches/1,778–2,540 centimeters of snow *annually!*). Many of the other glaciers in the park spill right into the sea, where the churned-up water caused by their "calving" creates a rich marine environment haunted by great numbers of fish, seals, sea otters, and whales. Towering above all this activity, sheer cliffs line the great fjords that have been carved out of the coastline by glaciers which have since stopped retreating.

The park's *Visitor Center* is located in downtown Seward on 4th Avenue. Here you can see a variety of exhibits illustrating the natural history of the park, as well as an excellent audio-visual show on its wildlife and scenic beauty. The best way of seeing the much-indented coastline of the park is to take a flightseeing or charter boat tour from Seward; kayaks can also be rented in town, but the coastline here is completely exposed to the Gulf of Alaska, and dangerous storms can blow up in a hurry. (For more information, contact the Seward Chamber of Commerce, Box 749, Seward, AK 99664.)

The only overland access to the park is via a short spur road north of town that leads to the *Exit Glacier.* You can walk to the foot of this gleaming whitish-blue glacier, which flows down from the Harding Icefield, from the end of the road, but you're best advised to stay off its dangerously unstable ice. (Ranger-led hikes and programs available in summer.)

To continue on this route, follow the Seward Highway north to *Tern Lake Junction* (165 miles/265 km. from Anchorage) and then turn left onto Highway 1, which from this point to its southern terminus in Homer is called the Sterling Highway. The road at this point heads due west through the valley of the *Kenai River,* the most heavily fished river in the state. Chances are you'll see moose—which grow to impressive proportions in the ideal habitat of the peninsula—going about their

Moose on the Kenai Peninsula

business in swampy, low-lying areas. For much of its east-west distance, in fact, the Sterling Highway crosses the forested, lake-studded plateau of the *Kenai National Wildlife Refuge,* a huge reserve that covers almost half the total area of the peninsula and provides prime habitat for moose, bear, Dall sheep, and a variety of other wildlife. The *Swanson River Road,* which will come up on your right at the 210-mile (338-km.) mark from Anchorage, heads due north into the heart of the refuge and is an excellent jumping-off point for canoe trips of varying length in this beautiful wilderness region. (See page 78 for the address of the refuge office, which will be happy to provide you with information on canoe trips in the region.)

Soldotna (221 miles/356 km. from Anchorage) didn't even exist 50 years ago; today, it's the commercial hub of the peninsula, with a "strip" that is typical of many of

Alaska's roadside communities, as well as the seat of the borough government and headquarters for the Kenai National Wildlife Refuge. And if you suddenly find yourself overcome by the urge to do battle with an 80-pound king salmon, Soldotna and the Kenai River will prove ready and willing to aid you in your quest; you'll find close to a dozen guide and charter outfits in town waiting to serve you.

There are two roads that lead from here to **Kenai,** the peninsula's oldest and largest community: the Kenai Spur Road (also known as the Soldotna Y), or the Sterling Highway via the Kalifornsky Beach Road. Both are around 10 miles (16 km.) long, with the latter just a bit longer and a tad more scenic.

Built by the Russians as a fur-trading post in 1791 and named Fort Nicolas, the settlement was renamed Kenai and soon became the center of the Russian Orthodox church in Alaska after a mission was established here in 1846. Oil and gas development in Cook Inlet since the 1950s has spurred the growth of the town, and today there are 15 drilling platforms in the inlet, as well as two refineries, a gas liquification plant, and a chemical/fertilizer plant north of town.

The best-known structure in town, however, is the pretty blue-and-white *Holy Assumption Russian Orthodox Church* with its three onion-shaped domes. Built around the turn of the century to replace the original mission church, it is now the oldest Russian Orthodox church in Alaska and listed on the National Register of Historic Places. Inside you can see a number of valuable old icons, as well as a 200-year-old Bible brought from Czarist Russia by way of Siberia (conducted tours are given by the resident priest).

The area around the church, much of it now abandoned, is known as *Old Town* and includes the *Fort Kenay Museum.* From the bluff overlooking the mouth of the Kenai River nearby, the view extends over the deep-blue waters of Cook Inlet to the summits of the volcanic Aleutian Range on the other side. In clear weather you can't miss the snow-capped cones of *Mount Redoubt* (10,197 feet/3,108 meters) and, farther to the south, *Mount Iliamna* (10,016 feet/3,063 meters).

From Kenai the route returns to Soldotna and then heads south along Cook Inlet on the Sterling Highway. The views of sandy beaches, blue water, and the distant Aleutian Range will be spectacular on clear days, and you'll pass a number of picnic areas where you can stop and savor them. The beaches on this side of the peninsula are also famous for their yield of tasty razor clams (licenses available at most sporting goods stores, with a bag limit of 60 in effect at all times). There's another handsome Russian Orthodox church above a small fishing harbor at *Ninilchik* (282 miles/455 km. from Anchorage), and visitors are welcome as long as they stick to the path leading up to it from the store below.

Homer (320 miles/516 km. from Anchorage), the final stop before you return to Anchorage, lies at the end of the Sterling Highway on the shores of *Kachemak Bay*, a beautiful 30-mile-(50-km.-) long inlet at the southwestern tip of the Kenai Peninsula. Besides being a busy commercial fishing port, Homer, with its relatively mild climate (summertime highs average about 68°F/20°C and wintertime lows rarely drop below 0°F/−18°C), has more recently become a favorite resort and retirement community with Anchorage residents. You may take this as a sure sign that it has more than just breathtaking scenery going for it, although it has that in abundance. The Kenai Mountains and glaciers of the Harding Icefield dominate the horizon to the east and northeast, and the icy blue waters of the bay and Cook Inlet do the same to the south and southwest. Here, not surprisingly, you can enjoy the kind of activities that make a trip to Alaska's Southcentral region so memorable—beachcombing along all-but-deserted shores, flightseeing excursions to inaccessible glaciers, and superb deep-sea fishing (especially for halibut) in steep-sided fjords. At the same time, Homer is a surprisingly sophisticated community (for a small town in Alaska), with a good many art galleries and craft shops.

Finally, there's the *Homer Spit*, a narrow 5-mile-(8-km.-) long finger of gravel that juts into the bay from the southern end of town. In a sense, the Spit is to Homer what Sausalito once was to San Francisco (before it became fashionable and overly self-conscious)—a funky mélange of commercial and charter fishing outfits, arty shops and cafés, and fun-loving campers who pitch their tents right on the beach. It's an unlikely combination—and one unique to the Spit in Alaska—but somehow it works, lending the town a good deal of its charm in the process.

For a different perspective of this community on the Spit, be sure to take a spin on *Skyline Drive*—especially if it's a clear night—which runs along the bluffs behind town. Spread out below will be the arching finger of gravel, the cluster of lights at its tip, and, looming in the distance, the glaciated peaks of the Kenai Mountains. Perhaps no other vantage point in the state more perfectly and hauntingly illustrates man's rather tenuous foothold in the Alaskan wilderness.

Many summertime visitors to Homer take advantage of the Alaska Marine Highway System's twice-weekly runs to *Seldovia*, a tiny community situated on the craggy, much-indented shore of Kachemak Bay. Originally founded by Russian fur trappers in the 18th century, today Seldovia is a friendly town of some 700 people that has managed to preserve much of its old-time Alaskan charm. There are also a number of spots you can drive to outside of town that are both magnificently scenic as well as virtually unvisited by other human beings. If, on the other hand, you don't mind sharing them with people, the same kind of views and scenery— including (on a clear day) Mount Redoubt, Mount Iliamna, and 75 miles (120 km.) to the southwest, Mount Augustine (which was active as recently as 1986, depositing a layer of dust and ash onto both Homer and Seldovia)—can be enjoyed from the decks of the *Tustumena* as it makes its way across the mouth of Kachemak Bay.

Finally, for the true wildlife lover, Homer is the most popular base for excursions to the *McNeil River State Game Sanctuary* (see page 8). Every summer the world's largest concentration of grizzly bears gathers here near the mouth of the McNeil River to feed on the salmon that try to migrate upstream over a series of low but troublesome waterfalls. This, too, is a unique spectacle—although of an entirely different sort—and one that state wildlife officials are determined not to interfere with: Permits to visit the sanctuary during the peak spawning season must be applied for by mail, and are limited to just ten a day. (For further information, contact the Alaska Department of Fish and Game, 333 Raspberry Road, Anchorage, AK 99502.)

To return to *Anchorage,* the starting point of the route, follow the Sterling Highway north out of Homer. The trip, all of it on well-maintained Highway 1, is approximately 226 miles (365 km.), and can easily be done in a day.

TRAVEL ROUTE 3: Southeastern Alaska's Glaciers and Fjords: Prince Rupert–*Sitka–Juneau–*Skagway–Whitehorse

See map on page 87.

Alaska's Panhandle (or "Southeast," as its residents prefer to call it), a magnificently beautiful region of lonely islands, precipitous fjords, and soaring mountains, stretches some 500 miles (800 km.) from Yakutat Bay in the north to the Portland Canal in the extreme southeastern corner of the state. Much of it—more than 90 percent, in fact—is owned by the United States government and has been set aside as national parkland, monuments, and forests. This expanse includes the Tongass National Forest which, at almost 17 million acres, is the largest national forest in the country. At the same time, its thousands of bays, coves, sounds, and straits are home to an abundant food supply that serves as the basis for an incredibly rich marine ecosystem. Salmon, halibut, black cod, herring, steelhead, trout, grayling, shellfish, humpback and killer whales, dolphins, sea lions, seals, and, most conspicuously, bald eagles (the region is home to the largest population of these magnificent raptors in the world) all thrive in or near the cold waters of the Panhandle. Its countless forested islands are prime habitat for Sitka black-tailed deer, black bear, and wolves, while its larger islands, such as Admiralty, Baranof, and Chichagof, support large numbers of brown grizzly bears and scattered populations of moose.

Almost all of the Panhandle region lies within the traditional territory of the Tlingit Indians, who, before the coming of the white man, had developed an advanced culture of their own. As was the case throughout the Americas, many of the towns in southeastern Alaska and northwestern Canada were originally settlements established by the region's indigenous people (including the Tsimshian and Haida Indians, in addition to the Tlingit). At the time, the Tlingit were noted for their skill in carving, and their powerful, somehow haunting totem poles were the most striking achievements of Northwest Coast Indian culture. Predictably, however, the economic activities and cultural attitudes of the white man eventually had a devastating impact on the native tribes of the region. It was only after their very survival was threatened by disease and cultural encroachment in the 19th century that the Tlingit were able to rebound, thanks in part to the efforts of a handful of anthropologists, concerned government officials, and native rights activists. Today they number over 10,000, and their glorious past is on display in museums and totem pole parks throughout the region. More important, however, are the tangible signs of their ongoing cultural revival (albeit with concessions to the 20th century)—encouraging proof that the European and Native American world views are not necessarily fated to be in opposition until the day the former "subdues" the latter, at the expense of one more piece of the world's cultural jigsaw puzzle. (For a more detailed look at Tlingit culture, see page 27.)

Perhaps the most significant feature of the Panhandle—at least in the eyes of a first-time visitor from the Lower 48—is the conspicuous absence of roads of any kind along its rugged and much-indented coast. As a result, boats and small aircraft are the primary means of transportation between the region's 20 or so settlements and larger communities. In addition, a variety of U.S. and Canadian companies run summertime cruises to southeastern Alaska. On the other hand, if you're traveling on your own, the best way to get around Southeast is via the state ferry network, also known as the Alaska Marine Highway System. The modern car ferries of the Marine Highway System provide regularly scheduled service from Seattle and Prince Rupert, British Columbia (with connections to the B.C. ferry system) to Skagway and points in between. Early booking is advisable, however (see page 123 for details).

Travel Route 3, which starts at Prince Rupert, British Columbia, follows the ferry route north through the famous Inside Passage. Along the way, hundreds of densely wooded islands, pristine bays, and snow-covered mountains provide a breathtaking and constantly changing backdrop for the attractive little towns (described below) where the ferries put in. From some of these towns you'll have a choice of side trips to a variety of scenic wonders, including the Mendenhall Glacier, the Juneau Icefield (the largest glacial accumulation in the world outside of Greenland and Antarctica), and, the high point of any vacation to Alaska's Panhandle, Glacier Bay National Park. At the northern end of the route is the historic gold-rush town of Skagway, with its charmingly restored Main Street district, as well as the infamous Chilkoot Trail, which was used by thousands of turn-of-the-century gold-seekers desperate to reach the Klondike gold fields in Canada's Yukon Territory.

Traveling time alone for the route, combining both ferry and car, amounts to 2 and one-half days. How much longer it actually takes will depend on the number of stop-overs you make, the amount of time you spend at each place, and the ferry timetables themselves.

Prince Rupert (population 25,000), the terminus for the B.C. ferry system and the port of embarkation for ferry service to Alaska, is Canada's second-largest port on the Pacific (after Vancouver), as well as the self-styled "Halibut Capital of the World." The town was founded in 1906 as the terminus of the Grand Trunk Pacific Railway and named in honor of Prince Rupert (1619–1682), cousin of King Charles II and one of the founders of the Hudson's Bay Company. Today, it is the world's most modern coal-handling port, exporting coal from Alberta to the "Pacific Rim" countries of Asia.

All over town you'll see beautifully carved totem poles. Adjoining the *Information Centre* is the *Museum of Northern British Columbia,* which documents the cul-ture of the Tsimshian Indians as well as the pioneering history of the region. In addition, on a clear day it's worth taking the train just outside the town to the summit of *Mount Hays.* From the top, there are sweeping views over the lush islands and towering mountains of northern British Columbia.

Prince Rupert itself is situated on an island, though you may not realize it until you see *Butze Rapids,* 4 miles (6 km.) from downtown. The swirling "rapids" here occur every six hours, caused by the changing tides in the narrow strait between the mainland and *Kaien Island,* on which the town is built.

Five miles (8 km.) east of town is *Oliver Lake Provincial Park,* which has a distinctive ecology all its own. The heavy rainfall totals in the park have given rise to areas of swamp up to 65 feet (20 meters) deep in rock cavities with no drainage outlet, in which centuries' worth of organic material has accumulated. The resulting lack of oxygen means there is practically no decay, and the soil is consequently lacking in nutrients. This anomalous environment produces stunted pines that grow to a height of only 10–13 feet (3–4 meters), even though they may be 150 years old—a kind of natural bonsai tree.

From Prince Rupert you can make a side trip to the **Queen Charlotte Islands,* one of the most remote and beautiful wilderness regions in all of North America, 50 miles (80 km.) west of the mainland. Named after Queen Charlotte (1744–1818), wife of George III, the archipelago today is home to the Haida Indians, once a warlike tribe but now renowned for their carving.

Graham and *Moresby Islands* are the two largest of the more than 150 islands in the group; like the others, each is an animal paradise, supporting large colonies of waterfowl and shore birds, bald eagles, deer, and, in the cold, clear coastal waters, an abundance of marine life.

From Prince Rupert you can take the B.C. ferry (advance booking is necessary for automobiles) to the little part of *Skidegate,* or to the largest town in the group, *Queen Charlotte City* (population 3,000), on Graham Island. The *Queen Charlotte Islands Museum* in Skidegate, an old

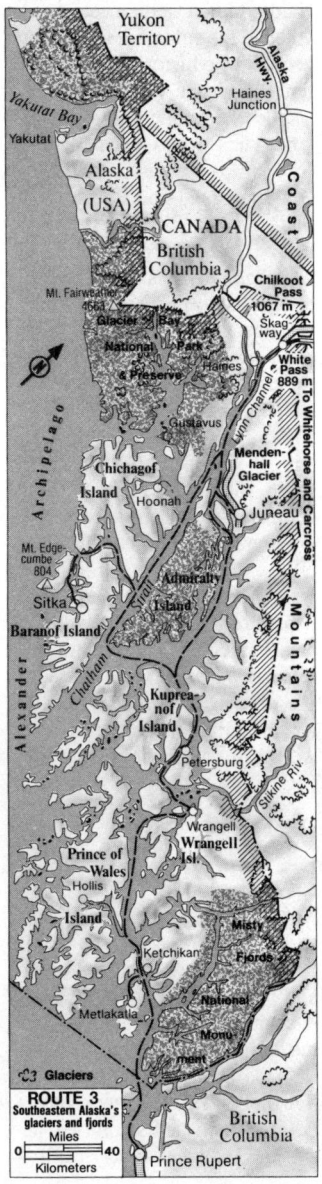

ROUTE 3
Southeastern Alaska's glaciers and fjords

Haida Indian settlement, is devoted to the culture of these proud people, who historically have suffered much abuse.

The one public road on the islands runs from Queen Charlotte City to *Masset,* a fishing village on Graham Island's north coast. The more remote parts of the archipelago (like much of the region encompassed by this route) can only be reached by plane or boat, unless you are a well-equipped hiker. (*Naikoon Park,* at the northeastern tip of Graham Island, has a short stretch of road at its northern end.)

Moresby Island, the long island with the rugged coastline to the south, has been the subject of controversy for years between logging companies and environmentalists. The logging companies want access to the island's expanses of virgin forests, while the environmentalists want to make it into a new national park in order to preserve its magnificent fjordlike terrain and colonies of sea lions, as well as its bald eagle nesting sites.

*

Ketchikan (population 8,000), situated on *Revillagigedo Island* (say "Rehvilla"—the locals do) and the Tongass Narrows, is Alaska's fourth-largest city and most southerly port, a 40 hours' sail from Seattle, Washington, and five hours from Prince Rupert, B.C. Established centuries ago as an Indian fishing camp—

Kichxaan is the Tlingit word for "salmon stream"—it had grown to become Alaska's busiest salmon-fishing port by the 1930s, with over a dozen salmon canneries in operation. Overfishing, however, led to a sharp decline in the salmon stock and harvests, and by the 1940s, the commercial fishing industry was on the skids. What could have been a disastrous situation for the town was prevented, fortunately, by stepped-up logging activity in the area. Today, logging and the revived salmon industry are largely responsible for the economic vitality of this rustic blue-collar town.

Ketchikan also benefits from a brisk summer tourist season, and boasts a number of attractions of interest to visitors. The old harbor quarter on *Creek Street,* for example (located at the opposite end of town from the state ferry terminal), was once Ketchikan's red-light district and still preserves much of the charm and color of those pioneering days. Because it is strung out between the narrows on one side and the steep slopes of Deer Mountain on the other, building space has always been at a premium here. As a result, many of the houses in town, like those along Creek Street, are built on stilts over the water or carved into the wooded slopes of the mountain, and accessible by long wooden staircases or winding streets. On the boardwalk facing the southern bank of Ketchikan Creek you'll find Alaska's only brothel-cum-museum, *Dolly's*

House, which, like a number of other turn-of-the-century structures in town, has been painstakingly restored. For those with a thirst to learn what Ketchikan's residents do for relaxation these days, there are a number of dimly lit bars in the old waterfront area nearby where fishermen, loggers, and Indians hobnob after hours.

The revival of the salmon industry is due in part to the establishment of a number of fish hatcheries in and around Ketchikan. The *Deer Mountain Hatchery,* on the other side of Ketchikan Creek (opposite the Totem Heritage Cultural Center, see below), is one of these, and is open to the public daily during the summer. The observation platforms at the hatchery are the best places to watch the thousands of salmon in the creek during the spawning season.

No visit to Ketchikan would be complete without taking the time to check out the cultural legacy and woodcarving skills—both past and present—of the area's Tlingit, Haida, and Tsimshian Indians. The *Totem Heritage Cultural Center* (601 Deermont Street) has a display of 33 totem poles from the second half of the 19th century—the largest collection of unaltered poles in Alaska. *Saxman Totem Park,* on the other hand, which is located 4 km. (2.5 miles) south of town in the Tlingit village of Saxman, boasts over 20 "modern" totem poles, many of them created by master carvers who teach their craft to willing students within the confines of the

Totem pole in Totem Bight Park

park. (They'll also be happy to carve you a personalized totem pole—at a cost of a couple of thousand dollars a foot.) The most attractive display of totem poles in the area, however, is to be found at **Totem Bight State Historical Park,* located 10 miles (16 km.) north of town on a small promontory overlooking the coast. Here, in a lovely setting framed by dense forest, you can see 13 totem poles and an authentic Tlingit tribal house that was erected in the late 1930s by the Civilian Conservation Corps—part of a larger preservation project that was never completed. (For more on the history and symbolism of totem poles, see page 27.)

From Ketchikan you can take a little ferry to *Metlakatla* on Annette Island, a Tsimshian Indian village founded by the Anglican missionary William Duncan in 1887 as a model religious community.

Ketchikan is also the gateway to the *Misty Fjords National Monument,* the second-largest wilderness area in the United States, located just 30 miles (48 km.) east of town. Created by massive glaciers that ground their way down to the sea from the Coast Mountains tens of thousands of years ago and then retreated, Misty Fjords is famed for its sheer cliffs, deep canals, dense coastal rain forests, and plunging waterfalls. At times, it seems to be a place *out* of time; a place where it wouldn't be the least bit surprising to encounter a water-loving dragon, or an ornery troll guarding a narrow path through the forest, or any variety of mythological creatures your fantasy may indulge. Of course, there are no dragons or trolls here—just one magnificent species of mammal after another, including black and brown bears, mountain goats, moose, wolves, wolverines, martens, otters, sea lions, seals, porpoises, and whales. The abundance of bird and fish species is just as impressive, making it one of the most diverse and productive ecosystems in all of North America. Most visitors to the monument, however, come to soak up some of its spectacular scenery, as well as to lose themselves, if only temporarily, in an exotic landscape that is as far removed from the noise and con-

gestion of modern urban living as any place can be. The aura of magic and mystery that is so tangible here undoubtedly owes much to the misty low-hanging clouds that pile up against the towering wall of the Coast Mountains, cloaking in invisibility what was vividly real only seconds before. And yes, those clouds also mean that this part of the state gets more than its fair share of precipitation—over 170 inches (432 centimeters) in a typical year, much of it falling as a mistlike drizzle (hence the name). Don't let that discourage you, however: For those of you with a love of unspoiled wilderness, a romantic imagination, and a good raincoat, a trip to Misty Fjords will pay spectacular dividends on your investment of time.

Day-long boat and flightseeing trips to the monument leave Ketchikan every morning. (Some of the cruise lines also include it on their itinerary.) For the more adventurous, the U.S. Forest Service maintains 14 cabins (each one sleeping six), most of them in highland areas, and 20 miles (32 km.) of trails in the monument. (For additional information, contact: Misty Fjords National Monument, P.O. Box 6137, Ketchikan, AK 99901.)

*

Wrangell (population 2,400) sits at the northwestern tip of Wrangell Island, just 7 miles (11 km.)

south of the mighty *Stikine River.* Founded in 1834 by the Russians and named Redoubt St. Dionysius, it was then leased to the Hudson's Bay Company from 1840 until 1867, at which point it passed into the possession of the United States along with the rest of Alaska. Today, Wrangell is an unassuming and friendly town, most of whose residents either fish or log commercially. Its principal attraction for visitors is *Chief Shakes Island,* an islet in the well-protected harbor. It features a number of Tlingit totem poles and a reconstruction of a Tlingit community house complete with authentic native tools and furnishings. In town, the *Wrangell Museum,* located in an old schoolhouse just down the road from the ferry terminal on 2nd Street, has displays of Indian canoes, jewelry, and other crafts, as well as a variety of exhibits illustrating the history of white settlement of the area. The *Bigelow Museum,* on Stikine Avenue, has a good collection of antiques and memorabilia from pioneering days; it is open when cruise ships or ferries are in town, or by special request.

Wrangell is also a favorite base for excursions on the Stikine River, the fastest navigable waterway on the continent. It offers first-rate canoeing, kayaking, and rafting for thousands of river enthusiasts every year. As the only navigable waterway into the Canadian interior between Ketchikan and Skagway, it has been used by the Indians of the region for centuries as a primary transportation route. The most popular starting point for trips by river sports enthusiasts is *Telegraph Creek,* British Columbia, about 150 miles (240 km.) upstream from the river's mouth. (The 55-mile-/88-km.-long canyon directly above Telegraph Creek is among the wildest stretches of white water in the world.) From there, it's an easy ride, with magnificent scenery and countless channels to choose from all the way down to the river's mouth. (Contact the Wrangell Chamber of Commerce, P.O. Box 49M, Wrangell, AK 99929 for further information.)

Continuing north from Wrangell, the ferry will make its way through the once-dreaded *Wrangell Narrows.* Nowadays, thanks to a modern system of beacons and buoys, the narrows no long terrify navigators.

Coastal scene, Wrangell

After a four-hour sail, the ferry comes to **Petersburg** (population 3,000), at the northern end of the narrows. It would be natural for you to assume that the town was named for the Russian czar who encouraged the early exploration of Alaska; but, in fact, it is named after Peter Buschmann, the Norwegian who founded it in 1897. Buschmann was attracted to the spot by the rich fishing grounds of the Inside Passage, the availability of wood and ice (from the nearby LeConte Glacier), and the natural harbor provided by the site. He soon had built a salmon cannery (the forerunner of today's Icicle Seafoods Inc.) In time, Buschmann was joined in his saltwater paradise by a number of his countrymen, and over the ensuing decades a little Norwegian colony sprouted and flourished here.

This Scandinavian legacy is still very much a part of Petersburg's appeal and continued prosperity, and every year its residents honor that heritage by celebrating Norwegian Independence Day on the weekend nearest May 17. In addition, many of the town's buildings are decorated with *rosemaling* designs, the traditional Norwegian style of house painting—most notably the *Sons of Norway Hall,* a National Historic Site located in the heart of the waterfront district. A walk along Petersburg's busy harbor to the hall and picturesque *Hammer Slough,* just south of the post office, will present you with dozens of opportunities for picture taking;

the Coast Mountains provide a majestic backdrop for the handsome houses lining the way and the many fishing boats rocking in their berths. Best of all, after you've worked up an appetite, you can stop at one of the fine restaurants the town has to offer—fresh seafood, of course, is the local specialty.

Mitkof Island, on which Petersburg is situated, boasts one of the few roads in all of Southeast Alaska. The so-called Mitkof Highway leads 34 miles (54 km.) south from downtown Petersburg to the end of the island opposite the Stikine River delta; the first 17 miles (28 km.) are paved, at which point it becomes a well-maintained gravel road. Along the road are numerous spots where you can stop to try your luck with the local trout and salmon populations, enjoy a picnic, or simply revel in the solitude provided by the lush coastal forest. A local tree nursery and fish hatchery, both open to the public, are also of interest.

Petersburg is also an ideal point of departure for a day trip by plane or charter boat to the *LeConte Glacier,* the southernmost tidewater glacier in North America. The LeConte is also one of the most active glaciers on the continent, and "calves" large chunks of ice into its bay with noisy regularity. While these mini-icebergs can pose a problem for the kayakers who flock to the region's sheltered waterways during the summer months, they're a big hit with the

area's sea lion and seal populations, which use them in their own
inimitable way as floating chaise
lounges.

From Petersburg, the state ferries follow a twisting route north
and west toward Sitka, on the
western coast of Baranof Island.
In all probability, at some point
along the way you will suddenly
hear the cry, "There she blows!"
As you reach the rail of the ship,
you'll be greeted by one of the
most awe-inspiring spectacles in
Nature—the sight of **humpback
whales** breaching and frolicking
in the plankton-rich waters of the
Inside Passage.

Every year in early summer
about 2,000 of these magnificent
creatures travel from their winter
quarters off the coasts of Hawaii
and the Baja Peninsula to the
colder waters of the Gulf of
Alaska. Humpbacks, which are
dark in color, with white patches
on their fins and undersides, often
grow to more than 52 feet (16 meters) in length and top more than
40 tons in weight. When they dive,
their characteristic tail fins—no
two of which have the same mark-
ings, making it easier for scientists
to identify and track individual
whales—rise completely out of
the water, only to slap it with a re-
sounding clap as the whale slips
beneath the surface. Even this,
however, pales in comparison to
the sight of a particularly playful
whale—and humpbacks are playful creatures—leaping out of the
water as far as gravity will allow,
turning in mid-air as if to acknowl-

edge the gasps of his awe-struck
audience, and falling back again
with a mighty crash.

The humpback whale is also a
"musical" creature. Males of the
species, swimming at a depth of
anywhere between 100 to 165 feet
(30 and 50 meters), will "sing" to
gain the attention and win the favor of a female whale. According
to scientists, these "songs" are
made up of complex and constantly recurring themes that vary
from group to group. On some occasions, certain less musical
whales will resort to force when
courting, pushing better singers
away from females in order to
draw attention to themselves. This
type of behavior, however, corre-
sponds to the humpbacks' tenure
at their winter quarters, where
their mating takes place and baby
humpbacks, weighing as much as
a ton and a half, are born.

The humpback whale is an endangered species, and although
they've been protected around
the globe, their numbers—
estimated between 8,000 and
10,000 individuals—are slow to
increase. To allow these magnificent creatures to vanish from the
face of the earth would be a tragedy beyond measure. Fortunately,
the waters off the southern coasts
of Alaska continue to provide the
humpback with an excellent summer habitat in a safe and relatively
pollution-free environment. And
that's to our benefit, as well, for the
psychic rewards of watching a
family of humpbacks at play on a
sunny day in the waters of the In-

side Passage are likely to last as long as one retains the power of memory.

*Sitka (population 8,000), the oldest and most historic town in the Panhandle, has few rivals on the Pacific coast for sheer natural beauty. On clear days—of which, it must be confessed, there are not many (Sitka averages about 165 inches/420 centimeters of precipitation annually)—the views from *Castle Hill* over the harbor to the symmetrical volcanic cone of *Mount Edgecombe,* which is jokingly referred to as "Alaska's Mount Fuji," remind one of something out of an opera by Wagner or a Norse edda. It's enough to make you forget—at least for a little while—that the closest good-sized town in any direction is 90 miles (144 km.) distant—by *air,* no less (Juneau or Petersburg, take your pick).

And yet, in spite of its isolation, Sitka has attracted adventurous Russians and Americans for close to 200 years. The first European to cast his eye on the site was the Russian governor of Alaska, Alexander Baranof, who established a fortified trading post here in 1799. The area's Tlingit Indians, who had occupied the surrounding region for centuries, had other ideas, however, and burned the fort to the ground in 1802. Baranof returned to reestablish the trading post two years later, and succeeded in driving the Tlingits from the area for the next 20 years. By 1806, Sitka, or New Archangel, as it was called

then, had been named the capital of Russian America, and a ruthless trade in sea-otter furs soon made it a thriving and relatively civilized little town. Among other anomalies in early 19th-century Alaska, the handsome governor's palace (which later burned down) was finished as if it were a dacha outside of Moscow or St. Petersburg, and even boasted a library. The Russians' oasis in the wilderness slipped into a long decline, however, as the sea otter was hunted to the brink of extinction in the middle decades of the century and, later, the discovery of gold in the Interior drew the action elsewhere. By 1906, with Alaska a possession of the United States, Juneau had replaced Sitka as the territorial capital.

If the 19th century was rather unkind to the town, our own has been somewhat more generous. A salmon cannery that opened in the last decades of the 19th century managed to support Sitka through the long decades leading up to the Second World War. The war itself brought a substantial amount of military personnel and economic activity to town. After the war, fishing reasserted its dominance, with the role of logging and pulp operations becoming increasingly important. Today, as is the case throughout much of Southeast, logging and fishing continue to drive the local economy, with summer tourism contributing a nice bit of change to the mix.

The residents of Sitka are well aware of this fact, and do a great deal to show off their town and its colorful history to best advantage. The *Sheldon Jackson Museum,* on the campus of Sheldon Jackson College, for example, is one of the outstanding ethnographic museums in Alaska. Named for the peripatetic missionary who founded the school in the 1870s and gathered many of the articles exhibited himself, the museum is an unending source of delight for serious students of native Alaskan culture and laymen alike. Among its many interesting exhibits are examples of watertight clothing made from fish skins, pieces of woven war armor fashioned by the Tlingits, and a display of native means of locomotion, including an Eskimo umiak, an Aleut bidarka, an Athapaskan canoe, and a Tlingit dugout. The museum is open daily in the summer.

Heading west toward the harbor, you'll soon come to *St. Michael's Cathedral,* one of the finest onion-domed Russian Orthodox churches in Alaska. The church, which was built by Bishop Innocent Venyaminov in 1848, was the spiritual center of Sitka for more than a century. When it caught fire in 1966, its valuable old icons were saved by alert townspeople, thereby averting a total disaster. The rebuilt church, an exact replica of the original, was completed in 1976 and houses all of the rescued icons and art treasures from the first St. Michael's.

In addition to the views it affords of the harbor, Sitka Sound, and Mount Edgecombe, Castle Hill was also the site of the ceremony sealing the transfer of Alaska to the United States on October 18, 1867. The path to the historic hilltop site begins at the downtown post office on Lincoln Street.

At the opposite end of town, the *Sitka National Historical Park,* situated on a small promontory overlooking the Sound, encompasses the site of the old Tlingit village where the "Battle of Sitka" was fought in 1804. A *Visitor Center* offers an audio-visual show tracing the history of the town, as well as a few displays of relics from the battle. The *Southeast*

Totem poles

Alaska Indian Cultural Center is located in the same building, and encourages visitors to watch its many fine Tlingit artists and craftsmen as they work. In addition, there are a number of fine totem poles outside the Visitor Center and along the path leading to the site of the battle.

From Sitka, it's a long but breathtakingly scenic passage to *Juneau* (population 30,000), Alaska's capital and third-largest city.

JUNEAU

Situated on a strip of land flanked by the *Gastineau Channel* and the steep slopes of *Mount Juneau* (3,580 feet/1,090 meters), Juneau has been compared to San Francisco for its scenic beauty. Juneau has also been called the most beautiful state capital in the country. Heading up the narrow Gastineau Channel on a clear day, it's easy to see why: The rugged Coast Mountains, decked out in their lush coats of spruce and hemlock, and topped by sparkling white snowcaps, majestically stand guard over the city. Of course, a clear day in Juneau is often cause enough for celebration (the city averages about 92 inches/233 centimeters of precipitation annually), but don't let that discourage you; much of the really nasty weather is confined to the late fall and winter months, and even then, Juneau's cosmopolitan sensibilities are enough to cheer up the soggiest spirits.

The town was born in 1880 when two prospectors by the name of Joe Juneau and Dick Harris found traces of "color" in the small stream that now cuts through the center of town. Word of the discovery quickly reached Sitka, and the rush to "Harrisburg" was on (so-named at first, legend has it, because the other partner could neither read nor write his name). Eventually, all the digging and scraping in the valleys behind town uncovered a gold-bearing quartz lode that proved to be among the largest ever found in North America; thus, the future of the town was secured. (By the start of the Second World War, more than $150 million worth of gold had been recovered in the Juneau area.)

At almost the same time, another strike was made on Douglas Island, directly across the Gastineau Channel from Juneau. By the end of the 1880s, the Treadwell Mine and community of Douglas were serious rivals for the leading role in the regional economy. Juneau capitalized on its slight head start, however, and by 1906 had managed to attract the territorial government away from Sitka (a blow from which the latter never really recovered).

When the ore was finally mined out in the 1940s, Juneau fell back on its position as the territory's administrative center, and as the population of Alaska grew in the postwar years, so did Juneau. In the 1960s, the city of Juneau merged with Douglas, its old rival across the channel, as well as the Greater Juneau Borough, to create the City and Borough of Juneau— at 3,108 square miles (8,050 sq. km.) the largest city area in the Western Hemisphere, and the second-largest in the world (after Kiruna, Sweden).

Today, Juneau is an attractive and unhurried state capital, with over half its residents employed directly by government, and many of the others tending to the needs of those who are. In 1976, Alaskans decided that Juneau was too remote and inaccessible from the rest of the state, and voted to move the capital north to Willow, a little town north of Anchorage on the George Parks Highway (see page 56). What could have been a fatal blow to Juneau's continued prosperity and importance has instead become a sort of sword of Damocles, as Alaskan voters wrestle with the question of whether or not the state has enough money to finance the move. With North Slope oil production peaking, however, and industry plans to drill in the Arctic Wildlife Refuge under attack, it looks as if Juneau's position is secure for the foreseeable future.

Most of the city's sights can be seen in the course of a walk through the busy streets of the downtown area. Juneau's main shopping street, *Franklin Street*, leads past the **Red Dog Saloon.** Famous throughout the Great North during the gold rush era, this emporium can still pull off a passable imitation of a frontier-style bar. Continuing up Franklin, you'll soon come to **St. Nicolas Russian Orthodox Church** (1894), the oldest original Orthodox church in southeastern Alaska. Inside are a number of art and religious treasures dating to the 18th century.

The **Governor's Mansion,** at 716 Calhoun Avenue, is a handsome white colonial-style building that's visible from most parts of town. Unfortunately, it's only open to the public one day a year. For those who want to see the governor, you can catch him in action at the **State Capitol Building,** located at 4th and Main Streets, when the legislature is in session (January to May); during the summer, tours of the building are offered on the half hour, five days a week (and less frequently on Saturday).

Directly across the street is the **State Office Building,** which is affectionately referred to by locals as the "S.O.B." Inside, visitors will find the *State Library* and the *Alaska Historical Library,* in addition to a jumble of state offices and a light-filled main hall. Outside are fine views of the city, the Gastineau Channel, and Douglas Island to the west.

No visitor to Juneau should pass up the opportunity to stop in at the **Alaska State Museum,** located near the waterfront on Whittier Street. The collection of native artifacts is second only to Sitka's Sheldon Jackson Museum, and its other historical and taxonomic displays are also quite good.

Perhaps the most popular attraction Juneau has to offer, however, is the magnificent ***Mendenhall Glacier,** which ends at a small lake about 13 miles (20 km.) north of the city. It can be reached by car, bus, or bicycle. The glacier originates high in the Coast Mountains, about 12 miles (19 km.) from the *Visitor Center* at the lake, and is an offshoot of the mighty *Juneau Icefield* complex, which covers an area of some 3,850 square miles (10,000 sq. km.). (Other glaciers streaming down from the Juneau Icefield include the Taku, Eagle, and Herbert.) While it's possible to get a sense of the size and power of a glacier such as the Mendenhall on one of the guided hikes offered out of the Visitor Center (which also has a number of interesting displays on the flora and fauna of the region), the best way to see it is by plane or helicopter. Both are available in Juneau, and many of the helicopter tours offer the chance to land on a stable part of the glacier and allow you to do a little tentative exploring. Yes, it's expensive (anywhere from $100 to $150 for 45 to 75 minutes), but the experience is one you'll remember every time you toss an ice cube into a glass.

One of the most rewarding side trips you can make out of Juneau—indeed, one of the most spectacular in all of North America—is a day (or longer) excursion to ****Glacier Bay National Park and Preserve.** Barely 200 years ago, when Captain George Vancouver first sailed this way, what is now Glacier Bay was entirely clogged by a massive ice sheet spilling down from the St. Elias Mountains, over 100 miles (160 km.) to the north; in some places the ice was more than 4,000 feet (1,220 meters) thick. A little more than a century later, the ice had receded some 65 miles (105 km.) and exposed the bay— the most rapid retreat of a major ice sheet in modern times.

Today, 16 tidewater glaciers flow into the waters of the bay, choking it with ice floes large and small and creating a playground for marine wildlife that was, until recently, unsurpassed in North America. The hair seals are still here in great numbers, feeding on the abundance of fish in these frigid waters and seeming to delight in the almost non-stop show of calving glaciers. For some time, the overcrowding of the bay by eager tourists inhibited and caused a decline in the number of humpback whales who traditionally come here to feed; however, park officials have now taken measures to counter this by limiting the number of boats visiting the area between June and September. The land mammals, on the other hand, continue to thrive within the park's 3.3 million acres, and sightings of black and brown bears, mountain goats, moose, and deer are common. Likewise, the fishing and bird-watching within the park's boundaries are superb.

Glacier Bay is approximately 50 air miles (80 km.) west of Juneau and is serviced by a number of charter airlines, most of which fly to *Gustavus* (population 150) on the southern edge of the park. From Gustavus you can arrange for a charter boat excursion into the park or rent your own kayak with transportation provided to the launch point at *Bartlett Cove,* 10 miles (16 km.) into the park. If you're planning on staying overnight, you'll also find pleasant accommodations in town. (The backpacking in the park is outstanding, but the bear activity in certain areas can be high; check with the park rangers in Bartlett Cove before heading out.) Longer trips to the park must be booked well in advance, as must all the cruise lines. Flightseeing trips from Juneau, Haines, or Skagway, on the other hand, can be arranged on short notice. (For further information, contact the Superintendent, Glacier Bay National Park and Preserve, Gustavus, AK 99826. For further information on Glacier Bay tour operators, see the "Practical Information" section at the back of this book.)

Mountain-ringed **Haines** (population 1,200), the next stop on the route, is situated near the mouth of the Chilkat River, which pours into the beautiful *Lynn Canal,* a long narrow fjord that serves as the northernmost portion of the Inside Passage. Centuries ago, the site was occupied by Chilkat Indians, a branch of the Tlingit, who jealously guarded their route along the river leading into the interior—alas, to no avail. A Presbyterian mission was established here in 1881 (with financial help from Sheldon Jackson), and the discovery of gold in the Klondike less than 20 years later sealed the fate of the Chilkat village. The swarms of gold-seekers who found their way to the tiny settlement helped turn it into a thriving little port town, and in the process opened up the *Dalton Trail* over the Chilkat Pass (not to be confused with its more famous brother, the Chilkoot Pass) and Coast Mountains.

Today, the Haines Cut-Off (Highway 7) follows the old Dalton Trail northwest to the Alaska Highway, making it one of only three Panhandle communities connected to the Alaska Highway system (the others are Skagway and, far to the southeast, Hyder). If you decide to cut the route short here, or even if you're just spending the night, Haines boasts a number of interesting attractions.

Fort William H. Seward, once an old Army post, has been turned into an open-air museum and multi-use facility: some of the officers' housing has been converted into apartments, and two of the buildings on the grounds have been given over to the town's cultural activities. The *Alaska Indian Arts Skill Center,* in the former hospital building, is staffed by Tlingit artists who teach workshops in traditional Tlingit arts and crafts. Right behind it is the *Chilkat Center for the Arts,* housed in the former recreation hall and now converted into a

Bald Eagle

handsome theater and convention hall. The star attraction here during the summer months is the regionally acclaimed Chilkat Dancers, who preserve and perform many of the old Tlingit dances.

After most of the summer visitors have left, a new flock descends on the area—literally—around October. We're speaking, of course, of the bald eagles that find their way to the *Alaska Chilkat Bald Eagle Preserve,* about 20 miles (32 km.) north of town. Taking advantage of a stretch of the Chilkat River that stays open longer than the surrounding streams and rivers, the eagles—at times as many as 3,500—feed on spawned-out

salmon and fill the trees that line either side of the Chilkat for as far as the eye can see. The effect is at once inspiring, chilling, and even disconcerting—these are *eagles,* after all, not your garden-variety pigeon. For anyone in the area at that time of year, the spectacle is a must-see; for those who can't be there to see it in person, be sure to check out the film *Last Stronghold of the Eagles,* which is shown at the *Sheldon Museum and Cultural Center* on Main Street in Haines during the summer months.

As the ferry leaves Haines and heads north through the Lynn Canal, the thickly forested slopes of the Coast Mountains draw closer, the sounds of waterfalls tumbling down the sides of the steep valleys grow louder, and the glaciers on the mountain ridges high above seem to shimmer with a greater intensity. After an hour's sail, the engines are thrown into reverse as the ship nears the northernmost port on the Inside Passage, ***Skagway** (population 650), located at the foot of the precipitous Coast Mountains.

Don't let its size fool you. When the cruise ships are in town, Skagway can party with the best of them. Perhaps it's so spirited in summer because the town has to endure nine months of unassuming anonymity every year before it gets its chance to break out and entertain the outside world. Or maybe Skagway's penchant for high jinx goes back to the Klondike Gold Rush days, when, seemingly overnight, thousands of adventurers and speculators washed ashore on a tide of gold fever. In a matter of months, what had been a sleepy Tlingit village was transformed into a rollicking "metropolis" of 20,000, complete with enterprising saloon-keepers, store-owners, "party" girls, and wide-eyed prospectors, most of whom lost their shirts—and sometimes their lives—in this wild-and-woolly frontier town. At its peak, in 1898, Skagway boosters could point to its 19 restaurants, 15 general stores, 11 saloons, 9 hotels, 6 lumber yards, and 4 newspapers, among other things, as reasons why it was destined to become the greatest city of a great land. Five years later, it could claim barely 500 inhabitants, and only the freight traffic on the narrow-gauge railroad to Whitehorse, which opened in 1900, saved it from complete extinction.

Arctic Brotherhood Hall, Skagway

Much of *Broadway*, Skagway's main street, is now a National Historical Park. Among its many well-restored turn-of-the-century buildings is the *Arctic Brotherhood Hall*, whose false front is ornamented with over 20,000 small strips of wood, and the *Red Onion Saloon*, where sawdust on the floor substitutes for cuspidors, as it did in the days of the gold rush.

To get an even better sense of those colorful days, catch the "Skagway in the Days of '98 Show," a theatrical extravaganza featuring dance hall queens, ragtime music, and a rousing climax. It is staged (and has been for the last 60 years) every evening during the summer at the *Eagles Dance Hall*. Other diversions that attract locals and visitors alike include the *Gold Rush Stampede* in May; the *Summer Solstice Party* in late June; the Fourth of July festivities, which often run right into *Soapy Smith's Wake* on July 8; the 10-mile (16-km.) *"Hugs and Kisses" Road Race* in August; and the glorious *Skagway Street Gala* in September, which brings the curtain down on the town's public party season.

After all that fun, it's a wonder anyone has the energy to enjoy Skagway's spectacular natural surroundings. For those who do, however, one of the more popular activities is retracing the footsteps of the gold-seekers over the *Chilkoot Trail*.

During the few short years of the Klondike Gold Rush, some

A Klondike gold miner (1898)

trail from Skagway to Lake Bennett. Along its length, backpackers are treated to a majestic landscape of rain forest, ice-covered mountains, and beautiful Alpine lakes. The four-day hike is only for those who are both fit and properly equipped, however. The best time to hike the trail is during July and August, although even then you should be prepared for sudden snowstorms. In addition to a tent, sleeping bag, and food, essential items of equipment include foul-weather gear and mosquito repellent; it's also a good idea to have someone in your party carry survival equipment. Maps, weather reports, and general guid-

30,000 men and women made their way through the Coast Mountains and over the *Chilkoot Pass* (3,500 feet/1,067 meters), and then knocked together boats to continue their journey from Lake Bennett down the Yukon River to Dawson City. On average, it took them about three months to make the journey with their equipment and supplies—this in the depths of winter, no less, for the object was to reach the upper course of the Yukon in time to start work as soon as the ice broke up.

Today, the **Klondike Gold Rush National Historical Park,** which is administered jointly by the United States and Canada, takes in the whole of the

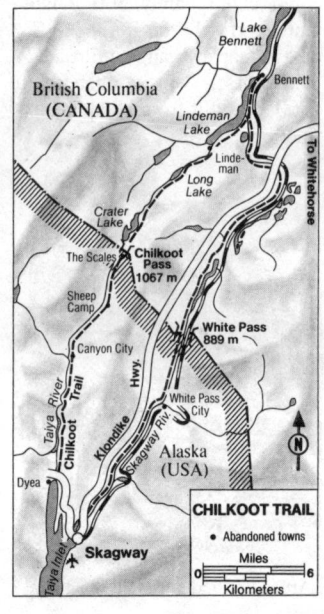

CHILKOOT TRAIL
• Abandoned towns

ance can be picked up at the *Park Visitor Center* in Skagway (Broadway and 2nd Avenue). You can also get information before leaving home by writing to the Supervisor, Klondike Gold Rush National Historical Park, P.O. Box 517, Skagway, AK 99840.

By calling ahead from Skagway, you can arrange for a boat to pick you up in Carcross at the end of the hike. Or you can walk along the railbed of the White Pass and Yukon Railroad to the Klondike Highway, on which buses to Skagway and Whitehorse pass with some regularity. And, if you decide in the course of your hike that you have what it takes to become a prospector, you can hire a canoe in Whitehorse and paddle down the Yukon: You still may be able to find an unstaked claim somewhere in the gold fields.

From Skagway, Travel Route 3 continues north on the Klondike Highway up the valley of the Skagway River. The steep ascent to *White Pass* (2,917 feet/890 meters) begins just outside of town; the railbed paralleling the highway for much of this stretch belongs to the White Pass and Yukon Railroad, which shut down its operations in 1982 for lack of business. To your right and left, waterfalls cascade over granite rock faces that have been worn smooth by ice. In the same stretch, the road passes in quick succession through a number of vegetation zones, from coastal rain forest to Alpine tundra on the pass.

The pass itself straddles the U.S.-Canadian border. On the other side of the border, you'll enter a different time zone, Pacific Standard Time, which is one hour ahead of Alaska Standard Time. The Klondike Highway continues down the eastern slope of the Coast Mountains, passing through a barren, wind-swept landscape characterized by long, narrow lakes, until it reaches **Carcross** (population 200), about 65 miles (105 km.) north of Skagway. The town, which grew up as a staging point for gold-seekers on the shallow stretch of water linking Lake Bennett with Tagish Lake, boasts the oldest hotel in the Yukon Territory, a crowded general store with an authentic old-time feel to it, and the *S.S. Tutshi,* an antique sternwheeler, now up on blocks.

For those who'd like to prolong their stay in Canada for a day or two, there's an enjoyable side trip from Carcross to **Atlin,* the northernmost town in British Columbia. To get there, follow the gravel Tagish Road east out of town until you reach *Jake's Corner,* a drive of 34 miles (54 km.). At Jake's Corner, turn right onto Highway 7, also known as the Atlin Road. The 60-mile- (97-km.-) long gravel road runs past a number of small turquoise-green lakes in which the wooded slopes of the

THE KLONDIKE HWY NO 2

surrounding hills are reflected on windless days.

This historic mining settlement of ***Atlin** (population 500) is nestled among the Coast Mountains on the shores of *Atlin Lake,* the largest natural lake in British Columbia (305 square miles/790 sq. km.), and likes to think of itself as "Canada's Switzerland." This lovely little outpost was originally a station on the telegraph line to the Yukon Territory, and time seems to have stood still in its streets lined by log cabins and Wild West-style façades. To this day it's inhabited by prospectors and trappers—as well as by artists who have retreated from the stress and hassles of modern civilization into the peace and quiet of this wildly beautiful land.

Lying as it does in the rain shadow of the mountains, Atlin is virtually guaranteed good weather during its hot, dry summers. It's also an ideal place from which to explore the glaciated Coast Mountains, either by bush plane or canoe (arrangements can be made once you get to town). For those who'd like to linger a day or two—or even a week—in this Shangri-la, Atlin offers a variety of accommodations from which to choose, most of them situated along the shore of its beautiful lake.

*

For those continuing on, the Klondike Highway heads north out of Carcross. Just past the junction with the Tagish Road will be a turnout and an informative plaque explaining the genesis of the Carcross desert to the east of the highway. This wind-scoured former lake bottom is the world's smallest desert, and has been designated an International Biophysical Programme site. Six miles (10 km.) farther north the road passes gorgeous *Emerald Lake,* whose greenish-blue water (an illusion created by light reflecting off the white sediment, or marl, of the bottom) is the delight of photographers.

The Klondike Highway joins the Alaska Highway 31 miles (50 km.) north of Carcross. From the junction it's just a few more miles to **Whitehorse** (population 15,000).

Situated on a low plateau overlooking the Yukon River, Whitehorse has been the capital of the Yukon Territory since 1953. It got its start, like so many towns in the region, as a staging point for prospectors on their way to the Klondike gold fields; but, unlike many of those same towns, its future was assured when the White Pass and Yukon Railroad, which had its terminus here, was completed in 1900. From Whitehorse, goods could be unloaded below the great rapids on the river and carried safely to Dawson City on large stern-wheelers. The construction of the Alaska Highway during the Second World War added to its importance, and it thereafter developed into the largest town in the Yukon Territory.

The *MacBride Museum,* on 1st

The *S.S. Klondike*

missions in the Yukon Territory. Finally, at the southern end of 2nd Avenue you'll find the ****S.S. Klondike,** one of the old stern-wheelers that plied the Yukon in the early years of the century.

From Whitehorse, you can extend your trip by turning north on the Alaska Highway and heading across the southwestern corner of the Yukon Territory and back into Alaska (see the Tok Cut-Off, on page 73 for further options); or you can turn south on the Alaska Highway and follow it to the junction just before *Watson Lake,* where the *Cassiar Highway,* which was completed in 1972, begins its 435-mile (700-km.) run through the virtually uninhabited northern half of British Columbia.

Avenue, with its displays of old gold-mining equipment and Indian arts and crafts, is a good place to spend a few hours reliving those days. The *Old Log Church* (Elliott Street and 3rd Avenue), which was built in 1900, now houses an exhibition on the history of Christian

The Cassiar Highway was originally a logging road linking the Cassiar asbestos mine with the

On the Cassiar Highway

port of *Stewart*. Today, it's a well-maintained all-weather road (half of it paved, half of it gravel) that follows the eastern flank of the rugged Coast Mountains. Along the way you'll find beautiful unspoiled wilderness provincial parks such as *Mount Edziza* and *Spatsizi*. (Organized raft trips on the Stikine River and hikes in the parks should be booked in advance.)

From *Meziadin Junction*, Highway 37A, otherwise known as the Stewart-Hyder Access Road, runs 42 miles (67 km.) through the Coast Mountains to those twin port towns at the head of the Portland Canal. Once-a-week ferry service to Hyder during the summer months connects it with the Alaska Marine Highway System.

For those continuing on to the Lower 48, the *Yellowhead Highway* (Highway 16) connects with the Cassiar Highway just south of *Kitwanga*, a Tsimshian Indian settlement. From there, your choices lead west 150 miles (240 km.) on the Yellowhead Highway along the Skeena River to *Prince Rupert* and the B.C. Ferry System; or east 857 miles (1,135 km.) to Edmonton, Alberta, and points south via Prince George, British Columbia.

Bush Alaska

As you surely realize by now, Alaska is a land of immense scale and proportions. It is almost impossible to get to know it well in a lifetime, let alone a single trip of a week or two. Part of this, of course, has to do with the fact that much of it remains inaccessible except by small plane or boat. That's the way most Alaskans like it, and the way it's likely to stay—at least for the foreseeable future. On the other hand, with the revolutions in transportation and communications technology that have occurred over the last 25 years, remoteness is no longer a valid excuse for ignoring the vast area known as "bush" Alaska—an area that embraces more than 75 percent of the state's total acreage.

Obviously, many travel professionals agree, and more and more of them are offering organized trips to some of these far-flung destinations. What follows is a brief description of five Alaska bush towns that serve as gateways to some of the most spectacular and pristine wilderness areas in the world (for a more detailed look at the regions and attractions referred to, see the "Getting Your Bearings" section at the front of the book). Although you *can* get to them on your own (by air from Anchorage or Fairbanks), your best bet is to join an organized tour, booked either before you leave home or a few days in advance once you get to Anchorage. (For more information on the major tour operators in and to Alaska, see the "Practical Information" section at the back of the book.)

While a trip to the Alaskan bush won't be everyone's cup of tea (and we trust those people know who they are before they find themselves a hundred miles from the nearest hot shower), the rewards, both physical and psychic, for those seeking a true wilderness experience, are likely to be beyond measure.

The *Kodiak Archipelago,* a cluster of some 200 islands located south of the Kenai Peninsula in the Gulf of Alaska, includes *Kodiak Island,* the largest island in the state (3,685 square miles/9,540 sq. km.), and the second-largest island in the United States (after the Hawaiian Islands' big island of Hawaii). Known as the "Emerald Isle" because of its lush forests, Kodiak Island was first explored by the Russian Stefan Glotov in 1763 and is the site of the oldest permanent European settlement in Alaska, founded in 1784.

The town of **Kodiak** (population 6,700) was established at the northeastern tip of the island in 1792 and quickly became its most important city (it was even the capital of Russian America for a time, until that distinction was transferred to Sitka in 1804). While the trade in sea otter pelts boomed, Kodiak thrived, but as those creatures were hunted to near extinction in the first half of the 19th century and gentlemen's fancies turned to other kinds of wardrobe accessories, the settlement found itself slipping into a long decline. It wasn't until the Second World War, in fact, that the outside world paid much attention to it, and then only as part of a first line of defense against a Japanese attack on the North American mainland. It made the news again in 1964, when the tidal wave generated by the Good Friday Earthquake leveled the town and destroyed its sizable fishing fleet—a disaster that even the resilient Kodiak Islanders had a tough time bouncing back from.

Through it all, however, both good times and bad, one thing has remained a constant here: its residents have always been able to depend on the rich waters of the Gulf of Alaska for sustenance and a living. Today, that's truer than ever before; Kodiak has become Alaska's principal commercial fishing port—and the second-largest in the United States—with its 2,000-vessel fleet harvesting the waters of the gulf for a variety of fish and shellfish, including salmon, shrimp, herring, halibut, whitefish, and Alaska's famous king crab (whose numbers, unfortunately, have dropped in recent years).

Where there are fish in Alaska, there are likely to be bears. Kodiak Island is no exception to that rule, and is, in fact, famous for its bears. Most of the island, as well as the other islands in the archipelago, are included in the 1.9 million-acre *Kodiak National Wildlife Refuge,* established in 1941 to protect the habitat of the Kodiak brown bear (a subspecies of the grizzly bear), the world's largest carnivorous land animal. These shaggy monsters—of which there are about 2,500 wandering the refuge, the highest density of brown bears in the world—can weigh as much as 1,500 pounds when fully grown, and subsist, for the most part, on huge quantities of fish and wild berries. (Thirty-three of the 50 largest brown bears ever taken in North America were from Kodiak.)

In addition to these awe-inspiring creatures, the refuge supports deer, elk, and a variety of fur-bearing mammals, as well as over 200 species of birds, and an abundance of fish. The hunting and fishing are excellent, as are more benign activities such as wildlife photography and bird-watching. There are any number of accommodations to choose from in the town of Kodiak (see the "Practical Information" section), and wilderness camping is allowed throughout the refuge. There are also nine public-use cabins scattered throughout the refuge, but reservations must be made in advance. For further information on the Kodiak National Wildlife Refuge, contact the Refuge Manager, 1390 Buskin River Road, Kodiak, AK 99615.

Before or after your wilderness adventure, be sure to spend a little time exploring the town of Kodiak. The *Baranof Museum,* located in an old warehouse that once was used to store sea otter pelts, is directly across from the state ferry dock. Here you'll find a collection of Koniag Indian artifacts, the archipelago's original inhabitants, as well as displays illustrating the history of the Russian settlement of the area. Behind it is the *Holy Resurrection Church,* with its characteristic blue onion domes, a reconstruction of the oldest parish church in Alaska. And, of course, you won't want to leave without having one last meal at one of its excellent seafood restaurants.

*

Located about 175 air miles (280 km.) west of Kodiak, **King Salmon** (population 400), on the north bank of the Alaska Peninsula's salmon-rich *Naknek River,* is just under an hour's flight from Anchorage. From here, it's a short floatplane hop to some of the finest salmon fishing in the world, not to mention spectacular wilderness scenery. Some of the better-known spots in the area include the lakes of the northern peninsula: Iliamna, Naknek, Becharof, and Upper and Lower Ugashik.

King Salmon is also the gateway to *Katmai National Park and Preserve,* which was established in 1918 to protect the ravaged yet eerily beautiful landscape created by the 1912 eruption of Mount Novarupta. The eruption, which was one of the most violent ever recorded in the northern hemisphere, shrouded Kodiak, 60 miles (100 km.) to the east, in showers of ash for the better part of two days. Striking evidence of the eruption can still be seen in the *Valley of Ten Thousand Smokes,* a barren valley, painted in a wide range of reds, browns, and ochers. The rivers fed by the snows of the Aleutian Range have cut spectacular canyons, some of them up to 650 feet (200 meters) deep, in the deposits of ash.

Accommodations are available in King Salmon, as well as nearby Naknek. Camping in the park is by permit only. For further information, contact the Superintendent, Katmai National Park and Preserve, P.O. Box 7, King Salmon, AK 99613.

*

Located about 320 miles (200 km.) west of the Alaska Peninsula in the Bering Sea, the ****Pribilof Islands** are composed of the main islands of *Saint Paul* and *Saint George* and three smaller islands. Regarded by naturalists and animal lovers alike as the "Galapagos of the North Pacific," these remote, wind-swept islands

Puffins

offer one of the great wildlife experiences in all of Alaska. Together, the islands are home to over 200 species of birds, including cormorants, kittiwakes, and puffins, and the seabird colony on Saint George Island, with over 2.5 million birds nesting on its cliffs every summer, is the largest such colony in the northern hemisphere. In addition, the islands boast the world's largest colony of fur seals, which were almost hunted to extinction in the 19th century. All these barking seals and flapping wings combine to create a spectacular display of Nature at her most prolific. Isolated, expensive to reach, and subject to frequent storms, the Pribilofs don't see many visitors (although that's changing).

For the relatively few who make the trip during the summer, however, it's an awesome experience.

There is direct air service from Anchorage to Saint Paul. Accommodations are available on either of the two larger islands—the Saint George Hotel on Saint George and the King Eider Hotel on Saint Paul (Saint Paul also has a limited selection of restaurants). For further information contact the Saint George Tanaq Corp., 2604 Fairbanks St., Anchorage, AK 99503; or the Tanadgusix Corp., P.O. Box 88, Saint Paul Island, AK 99660.

*

Far to the north and west, on the southern shores of the Seward

Peninsula, remote **Nome** (population 3,700) manages to maintain its spirit and sense of fun even as the winter storms off the Bering Sea try to erase it from the map. Maybe it's because Nome, more than most towns, knows firsthand just how fickle human nature can be. Founded in the winter of 1899, after gold was discovered in the streams flowing into Norton Sound, the fledgling town could claim more than 25,000 residents by the summer of 1900 (including a broken-down saloon-keeper by the name of Wyatt Earp), making it the largest, rowdiest—and last—of the great gold rush boomtowns. A few short years later, that number had dropped below 5,000, and in the decades that followed the population dwindled even further.

Today, the population of the town has stabilized around 3,700, and Nome has become the transportation and commercial center of the region, as well as a departure point for tours of the Eskimo villages of the Bering Sea Coast and wilderness trips to the extensive public preserves and refuges in northwestern Alaska. These include the *Bering Land Bridge National Preserve* on the Seward Peninsula itself; the *Koyukuk* and *Selawik National Wildlife Refuges* to the east; and the *Cape Krusenstern National Monument, Noatak National Preserve,* and *Kobuk Valley National Park,* all located above the Arctic Circle (for a more detailed description of this remote region see the "Getting

A traditional Eskimo sport

Your Bearings" chapter, pages 15–18).

In Nome itself, the *Carrie McLain Memorial Museum* boasts a wonderful collection of old photographs dating back to the gold rush days at the turn of the century, as well as exhibits devoted to the fauna of the Arctic tundra, the culture and lifestyles of the Eskimo, and the Bering Land Bridge.

Nome is also a town that likes a good party and doesn't need much of an excuse to hold one. Among its more noteworthy festivities are the Bering Sea Ice Golf Classic in March, the Memorial Day Polar Bear Swim, the Midnight Sun festival in June, the Anvil Mountain Run on the Fourth of July, and the Labor Day Bathtub Race. But its most famous party, and justifiably so, is held every year at the beginning of March for the finish of the world-famous *Iditarod Trail Sled Dog Race,* which ends in Nome after 1,049 grueling miles (1,678 km.). For further information about the sights and activities in and around Nome, contact the Nome Convention Visitors Bureau, P.O. Box 251–WMP, Nome, AK 99762.

Bush aircraft

*

Our last gateway destination is **Barrow** (population 3,000), on the shores of the Arctic Ocean, the largest Inupiat Eskimo community in the world and the northernmost settlement in the United States. Imprisoned by pack ice, sub-zero cold, and the long Arctic nights during the winter, Barrow is usually visited by outsiders during its brief "summer." But even then, with the sun hanging above the horizon continuously from May 10 to August 12, Barrow is an acquired taste. Most organized tours come so that visitors can stand on the edge of the continent north of town at *Point Barrow.* Other tour operators fly their curious adventurers east to the state-of-the-art industrial complex at *Prudhoe Bay.* And a few tour agents introduce their interested travelers to Eskimo culture, studiously explaining the adverse affects and impact that the modern world has had on the ancient subsistence lifestyle of the natives (which may strike some as contradictory). Not that an explanation is necessary: The less-than-easy coexistence of the two cultures is evident everywhere in Barrow. Don't be surprised if no one offers to rub noses with you in the traditional Eskimo form of greeting; at times it may seem as if even the huskies aren't particularly friendly. For further information on what to see and do in the Barrow area, contact the Barrow Convention and Visitors Association, P.O. Box 1060, Barrow, AK 99723.

Practical Information

This chapter is divided into two sections. The first, **General Trip Planning,** offers information you'll need for planning and researching your trip as well as guidelines on transportation to and around Alaska and other items of interest. (See listing in *Contents* for full range of subjects covered.)The second section, **Town-by-Town,** is organized alphabetically by town and provides information that will be helpful on site, such as local tourist offices, hotels, and transportation.

GENERAL TRIP PLANNING

Choosing When to Go. Alaska's dramatic coastlines, lush forests, and cloud-crowned mountains beckon to travelers willing to test their endurance in the wilderness, or those in need of some spiritual convalescence. The very vastness of this diverse land issues a challenge to the would-be explorer to delve into its reaches.

Summer is considered the high season in Alaska; the hospitable weather, which rarely descends below the 60s (15–20°C), makes camping and sightseeing a pleasure. In *June,* Ketchikan's King Salmon Derby engages some of Alaska's finest fishermen in well-beloved competition. (Not to be outdone, Valdez holds its Pink Salmon Derby later on in the month.) Fairbanks welcomes in the summer solstice with the unusual Midnight Sun Baseball Game. Other exciting summer events in *July* and *August* include the KSKA Bluegrass Festival in Palmer, the Alaska State Fair and Rodeo hosted by Haines, and the lively Blueberry Festival in Ketchikan.

Although Alaska's piercing cold scares off most vacationers during the wintertime, the season is peppered with winter carnivals, outdoor sports competitions, and enough sled dog races to distract your attention from bitter temperatures. *January* is the month for the Russian New Year and Masquerade Ball in Sitka, while *February* heralds in Anchorage's Fur Rendezvous, a tradition that harks back to the days when miners and trappers made their annual trip to Anchorage to trade and restock for the winter. Now this celebration focuses on sports contests, such as sledding and skiing, as well as an auto race and its tremendous fur auction. *March* brings the season's highlight, the challenging Iditarod Trail Sled Dog Race, a 1,049-mile (1,678 km.) solitary trek from Anchorage to Nome over tortuous terrain. Other cultural events during winter months include performances by the Fairbanks Symphony Orchestra in February, the annual Christmas Boat Parade in Sitka, and the Candle Lighting Service on the North Pole.

Although the weather is cool, spring and fall are also opportune times to journey to the Last Frontier. Hotel and lodge prices are reduced and crowds are diminished. One of the absolute "must-sees" during spring and fall is the enigmatic aurora borealis. This extraordinary occurrence (commonly known as the "northern lights") is a kind of mystical light show—brilliant, glittering bands of color whirl across the night sky. Autumn also brings the opening seasons of the Ketchikan Theatre Ballet, the Fairbanks Light Opera Theatre, the Anchorage Symphony Orchestra, and Juneau Dance Unlimited, as well as the joyous annual Athapaskan Old-Time Fiddling Festival in Fairbanks and Delta Junction's unique Emergency Medical Technician Winter Carnival. Another fall spectacle is the Quiana Alaska celebration in Anchorage, which features the retelling of Eskimo, Indian, and Aleut legends and traditional dancing in native costumes. This ritual serves as a reaffirmation of the solidarity of Native Alaskan culture. Spring's festivities range from the Savoonga Walrus Festival on St. Lawrence Island to the Little Norway Festival held in Petersburg to Nome's chilly Polar Bear Swim.

Climate. Alaska's monumental size prevents any uniform definition of its climate. Therefore, Alaska's general weather patterns are more easily classified when the state is partitioned into five distinct regions: southeast, southwest and the Bering Sea coast, southcentral and the gulf coast, interior, and the arctic.

Southeastern Alaska, also known as the "Panhandle," is distinguished by its abundance of glaciers, forests, mountains, and islands which form the Inside Passage. Ketchikan, Wrangell, Juneau, Sitka, Petersburg, and Haines are the major cities of the southeastern region. This area is tempered by the milder currents of the Pacific Ocean, resulting in high amounts of rain with overall moderate weather—at least by Alaskan standards. Temperatures in winter rarely dip below 20°F (-7°C), but precipitation ranges from 92 to 200 inches (24–508 centimeters) annually, depending upon the area. Summers are delightfully cool in the 60s (15–20°C), and may reach potential highs in the 70s and 80s (20–30°C).

Southcentral Alaska encompasses Anchorage and the Gulf Coast, and is sheltered by the Alaskan Range. The Gulf of Alaska delivers a high volume of precipitation to this region, and winter temperatures remain fairly consistent in the 20s (-10–0°C). Summers in southcentral resemble those in the southeast; they are agreeably cool, with temperatures ranging in the 60s and 70s (15–25°C).

Alaska's Interior, which includes Fairbanks, Delta Junction, Nenana, and Manley Hot Springs, may be considered the state's anomalous weather zone. Although this area receives very light precipitation, its temperature swings are staggering. It is unusual for winter highs to reach above freezing, and evening temperatures can fall to a frigid -50°F (-45°C). However, the opposite occurs during the summer when temperature readings often soar into the upper 80s and 90s (30–40°C).

Average Daily Temperatures

	January		February		March	
	F°	C°	F°	C°	F°	C°
Anchorage	13	−11	18	−8	24	−4
Barrow	−14	−26	−20	−29	−16	−27
Fairbanks	−13	−25	−4	−20	−8	−22
Juneau	22	−6	28	−2	31	−1
Ketchikan	34	1	36	2	39	4
Nome	6	−4	3	−16	7	−14
Petersburg	28	−2	31	−1	35	2
Valdez	25	−4	25	−4	30	−1

	April		May		June	
	F°	C°	F°	C°	F°	C°
Anchorage	35	2	46	8	54	12
Barrow	−2	−19	19	−7	−53	1
Fairbanks	30	−1	48	9	59	15
Juneau	39	4	46	8	53	12
Ketchikan	43	6	49	9	55	13
Nome	18	−8	36	2	45	7
Petersburg	40	4	47	8	53	12
Valdez	38	3	45	7	51	11

	July		August		September	
	F°	C°	F°	C°	F°	C°
Anchorage	58	15	56	13	48	9
Barrow	39	4	38	3	31	−1
Fairbanks	62	17	57	14	45	7
Juneau	56	13	56	13	49	9
Ketchikan	58	14	59	15	54	12
Nome	51	10	50	10	42	6
Petersburg	56	13	56	13	50	10
Valdez	56	13	54	12	48	9

	October		November		December	
	F°	C°	F°	C°	F°	C°
Anchorage	35	2	22	−6	14	−10
Barrow	14	−10	−1	−18	−13	−25
Fairbanks	25	−4	4	−16	−10	−23
Juneau	42	6	33	1	27	−3
Ketchikan	47	8	40	4	36	2
Nome	28	−2	16	−9	4	−16
Petersburg	44	7	36	2	31	−1
Valdez	39	4	30	−1	21	−6

Southwest Alaska encompasses the coastal plain area, the Bering Sea coast, and the Aleutian Islands. Winter temperatures here range from the minus teens to freezing (−28–0°C); summers are dry and mild, with temperatures settling in the 60s and 70s (15–25°C). The Aleutians remain a weatherman's enigma due to the radically changeable weather conditions that prevail. Plagued by heavy fog and rain, the islands are prone to unexpected, powerful windstorms called williwaws that create tremendous gales of wind.

The *Arctic* region, home of Kotzebue, Nome, Barrow, and Prudhoe Bay, is not quite as frigid as the legends would have you believe—but almost. High winds create the sharp, penetrating chill you feel, but actual winter temperatures do not usually drop below the minus teens (−30°C). Surprisingly, some areas of the Interior have colder weather than the Arctic region. Summers cannot be considered balmy by any standards, but they never fall below the 40s (4–10°C).

For more detailed information on climate, see pages 18–22.

Metric/U.S. Weight, Measure, Temperature Equivalents.

Throughout the text, measurements have been provided in standard U.S. linear form followed by metric equivalents in parentheses; likewise, Fahrenheit temperatures are followed by centigrade degrees. The following table is a quick reference for U.S. and metric equivalents.

Metric Unit	U.S. Equivalent	U.S. Unit	Metric Equivalent
Length		**Length**	
1 kilometer	0.6 miles	1 mile	1.6 kilometers
1 meter	1.09 yards	1 yard	0.9 meters
1 decimeter	0.3 feet	1 foot	3.04 decimeters
1 centimeter	0.39 inches	1 inch	2.5 centimeters
Weight		**Weight**	
1 kilogram	2.2 pounds	1 pound	0.45 kilograms
1 gram	0.03 ounces	1 ounce	28.3 grams
Liquid Capacity		**Liquid Capacity**	
1 dekaliter	2.38 gallons	1 gallon	0.37 dekaliters
1 liter	1.05 quarts	1 quart	0.9 liters
1 liter	2.1 pints	1 pint	0.47 liters

(*Note: there are 5 British Imperial gallons to 6 U.S. gallons.*)

Dry Measure		Dry Measure	
1 liter	0.9 quarts	1 quart	1.1 liters
1 liter	1.8 pints	1 pint	0.55 liters

To convert centigrade (C°) to Fahrenheit (F°):
C° × 9 ÷ 5 + 32 = F°.
To convert Fahrenheit to centigrade:
F° − 32 × 5 ÷ 9 = C°.

National Holidays. Listed below are the national holidays in Alaska. Specific dates for holidays may vary from year to year.

> New Year's Day (January 1)
> Presidents Day
> Good Friday
> Seward's Day (March 27)—marks the 1867 signing of a treaty whereby the U.S. purchased Alaska from the Russians; former Secretary of State William Seward strongly backed the proposal to buy Alaska
> Easter Sunday
> Memorial Day
> Independence Day (July 4)
> Labor Day
> Columbus Day
> Alaska Day (October 18)—celebrates the official transfer of Alaska to the United States
> Veterans Day (November 11)
> Thanksgiving Day
> Christmas Day (December 25)

During holidays, most places of business close, including banks, government offices, and many stores.

Time Zones. Most of Alaska is on Alaskan Standard Time (Yukon Time), which is five hours behind Eastern Standard Time and nine hours behind Greenwich Mean Time. Therefore, if it's noon EST in New York and Toronto, it is 7:00 A.M. in Anchorage. When it's noon GMT in London, it is 2:00 A.M. in Anchorage. There is a 17-hour time difference between Sydney, Australia and Anchorage; therefore, noon in Sydney translates to 4:00 P.M. the previous day in Anchorage.

Aleutian-Hawaii time applies to the western Aleutian islands of Adak, Atka, Attu, and Shemya, as well as St. Lawrence Island. The time zone is one hour behind Alaskan Standard Time.

Passport and Visa Requirements. If United States citizens intend to enter Alaska by way of Canada, they only need a current driver's license or another valid form of identification. Canadian citizens are not required to produce a passport or a visa to enter Alaska, but they should carry a driver's license or a proof of identification, such as a voter's registration card. British and Australian visitors must carry both a passport and one or two visas, contingent upon whether they enter Alaska by way of Canada.

Customs Entering Alaska. If you are not a U.S. citizen, then you must clear customs. Personal belongings to be used for professional or private purposes (i.e. jewelry, cameras, watches, radios, typewriters, etc.) do not have to be declared upon arrival in Alaska. This also covers all camping and fishing equipment, a two day supply of food, 250 grams of tobacco, and one liter of alcohol. Proof of registration for any guns brought into the state is mandatory. (Different restrictions apply to firearms brought in via Canada. Hunting equipment must be declared upon entry with a serial identification number. Contact a local Canadian Government Tourism Office for detailed information on prohibited firearms.) There is no limit on the amount of currency that you may bring into Alaska, although amounts over $5,000 should be reported to customs officials upon arrival.

Conversely, all visitors to Alaska, including U.S. citizens, must carry in at least $200 in cash to assure customs officials that you have adequate funds, as well a proof of return (i.e., an airline ticket).

Customs Returning Home from Alaska. To simplify passage through customs, it is wise for non-U.S. residents to carry copies of receipts for any items brought from home that were manufactured in the United States. This ensures you will not have to pay duty.

U.S. citizens returning from or entering Alaska via Canada should be aware of the restrictions pertaining to the importation and exportation of goods fabricated from endangered or extinct species. By-products constructed from their skin, fur, or bones, as well as walrus ivory, incur severe fines; you must obtain an export permit. Write to the U.S. Fish and Wildlife Service, 1011 East Tudor Road, Anchorage, AK 99503; tel. (907) 786-3311 or 1412 Airport Way, Fairbanks, AK 99701; tel. (907) 456-0239 for extensive information. You can also write to the Canadian Wildlife Service (c/o Convention Administrator, Environment Canada, Ottawa, Ontario K1A 0E7) for a specific listing of restrictions.

United States citizens who are returning from Alaska via Canada if they have been away for 48 hours may bring back $400 worth of goods duty-free. Exempt merchandise includes one liter of alcohol, 200 cigarettes, 100 cigars, or 250 grams of tobacco, and one bottle of perfume.

Australian residents may bring back $400 worth of duty-free purchases, as well as 250 grams of tobacco (or its equivalent in cigars or cigarettes), and one liter of alcohol.

British subjects are allowed a £32 limit on duty-free purchases, as well as 200 cigarettes, 100 cigarillos, 50 cigars, or 250 grams of tobacco, one liter of alcohol over 22% proof or two liters under 22% proof or two liters of table wine, 50 grams of perfume, and 250 grams of toilet water.

Canadians are entitled to $100 worth of duty-free purchases, or $300 worth if you have been out of the country for seven days or more. Duty-free items also include 250 grams of tobacco (or 200 cigarettes or 50 cigars) and one liter of alcohol.

Getting to Alaska by Air. *From the U.S.:* Domestic carriers flying to Alaska include Alaska Airlines, American Airlines, Delta, Hawaiian

Airlines, Northwest Orient Airlines, Trans World Airlines, and Western Airlines.

From the U.K.: You can fly non-stop on Aer Lingus, Air U.K., Birmingham Executive Airways, British Airways, British Midland, Brymon Airways, KLM (Royal Dutch Airlines), or Manx Airlines. You can also fly other airlines, such as Delta, KLM, SAS (Scandinavian Airlines), or Transavia Airlines, and make a connection in another European city before proceeding to Anchorage, Fairbanks, or Juneau.

From Canada: Trans North Air flies into Juneau from Whitehorse, and Trans Provincial Airlines flies into Ketchikan from Prince Rupert.

From Australia: Qantas Airways flies to Los Angeles, where you can take a connecting flight via Delta into Anchorage.

There is a staggering variety of ever-changing discount fares, hotel packages, fly-drive, and other deals that depend upon the travel season, the amount of time you wish to spend, the number of places you wish to visit, etc. Keep an eye on the advertisements in your newspaper's travel section and make your travel arrangements through a reliable agent or tour operator to get the best fares and packages.

Note: Always confirm both your departing and return flights at least 72 hours before your scheduled departure. Many airlines tend to over book flights, and it is always wise to double check.

Getting to Alaska by Boat. Many cruise lines offer package deals to Alaska from the United States or Canada; they usually run from May to September. Listed below are the names and addresses of some of the better-known cruise lines:

Admiral Cruises
1220 Biscayne Blvd.
Miami, FL 33101
tel. (800) 327-0271

Catamaran Cruise Lines
1620 Metropolitan Park Bldg.
Seattle, WA 98101

Costa Cruises
1 Biscayne Tower
Miami, FL 33131
tel. (800) 462-6782

Cunard Lines
555 Fifth Ave.
New York, NY 10017
tel. (800) 5- CUNARD

Exploration Cruise Lines
1500 Metropolitan Park Bldg.
Seattle, WA 98101
tel. (800) 426-0600

Holland America/Westours
300 Elliott Ave. West
Seattle, WA 98119
tel. (800) 426-0327

Princess Cruises
2029 Century Park East
Los Angeles, CA 90067
tel. (800) 533-1770

Regency Cruises
260 Madison Ave.
New York, NY 10016
tel. (212) 972-4774

Royal Cruise Lines
One Maritime Plaza
San Francisco, CA 94111
tel. (415) 956-7200

Royal Viking Tours
1 Embarcadero Center
San Francisco, CA 94111
tel. (800) 422-8000

Sea Venture Cruises
5233 NW 79th Ave.
Miami, FL 33166

Sitmar Cruises
10100 Santa Monica Blvd.
Los Angeles, CA 90067
tel. (800) 421- 0880

Society Expeditions
3131 Elliott Ave., Suite 700
Seattle, WA 98121
tel. (800) 426-7794

TravAlaska Cruise Tours
Fourth and Battery Building,
    Suite 808
Seattle, WA 98111
tel. (206) 441-8687

World Explorer Cruises
3 Embarcadero Center
San Francisco, CA 94111
tel. (800) 854-3835

Hotels and Other Accommodations. Wilderness lodges surrounded by splendid forests; private campgrounds a step away from the
heart-rending beauty of pristine rivers; exceptional hotels featuring fine
service and outstanding cuisine—these descriptions sketch only a few of
the options available for accommodations.

The Alaska State Division of Tourism (see page 134) offers free information concerning lodgings, which you can request through the mail.
We rank accommodations according to four categories: Luxury (🏠🏠🏠),
First Class (🏠🏠🏠), Second Class (🏠🏠), and Third Class (🏠); these ratings
correspond to the Alaska State Division of Tourism's classifications.
Luxury and First Class are delineated by three houses, a designation that
indicates the high quality of service and accommodations. The higher
prices for Luxury and First Class hotels are reflected in the amenities
they offer.

It is always advisable to book rooms in advance, especially during the
high season. During the peak travel season from late May through early
September, lodgings are often completely booked, and room rates soar.

Hotels and Motels. Outside of the main cities of Anchorage, Juneau, and
Fairbanks, first-tier hotels do not figure prominently in the state. However, there are many chain and privately-owned hotels and motels
throughout the state that provide good, comfortable lodging at reasonable prices. You won't find motels directly along the main roadways as a
rule; instead, roadhouses (simple inns) stand intermittently along the
main highways.

Bed and Breakfast Establishments. If you enjoy cozy surroundings in a private home at affordable prices, a bed and breakfast can prove a pleasant alternative to the anonymity of a hotel. "B & B" owners rent rooms in their homes on a daily or weekly basis, and frequently enjoy chatting with their guests, advising them of what to see and do in the area. Rooms may be small, but most come with the amenities of a hotel room. You may get the luxury of a private bathroom, but shared ones are liable to be the norm. The cost of the room includes breakfast at the house, which can range from coffee, tea, and toast to a full-blown meal of eggs, muffins with jam, and hearty sourdough pancakes.

Addresses of bed and breakfasts can be obtained from the local convention and visitors bureau or through the Alaska Bed and Breakfast Association, 3-6500-TP, Suite 169, Juneau, AK 99802, tel. (907) 586-2959, or Alaska Private Lodgings Bed and Breakfast, P.O. Box 200047-TP, Anchorage, AK 99520-0047, tel. (907) 258-1717.

Youth Hostels. Hostels provide basic temporary housing for students (and adults) at extremely low rates; approximately twelve hostels are located around the state. Accommodations vary, and it is always wise to bring a sleeping bag with you. Each hostel has its own regulations, which invariably includes guests assisting with daily chores.

Forest Service Cabins. Secluded and rough-hewn, these cabins are threaded throughout the Chugach and Tongass National Forests. Appealingly low priced (they run about $15 a night), they are ideal for reclusive vacationers who relish the pleasures of fishing, hunting, hiking, or just relaxing away from "the madding crowd." It may be necessary to charter a bush plane or boat in order to reach some of the more out-of-the way cabins. Be sure to come equipped with sufficient food and a bedroll and blankets. Due to the growing popularity of these cabins, it is necessary to make reservations at least six months in advance. Cabins may be rented for seven-day periods from April 1 to October 31 or for ten-day periods from November 1 to March 31. You can receive information about reservations from the Alaska State Division of Tourism, Tongass National Forest (Juneau Ranger District, 8465 Old Dairy Road, Juneau, AK 99801), or Chugach National Forest (Forest Supervisor, 201 East Ninth Avenue, Anchorage, AK 99501).

Wilderness Lodges. These hunting and fishing lodges are designed to immerse you in Alaska's extraordinary outdoors without the self-sufficiency required in the forest service cabins. A typical package deal for a week is relatively pricey, but it includes transportation to the lodge (via plane or private boat), accommodations and meals, as well as guided trips through the area. Arrangements can be made through the Alaska State Division of Tourism or your travel agent.

Also see the section called "Camping and Wilderness Exploration" beginning on page 126.

Currency. As one of the United States, the unit of currency in Alaska is, of course, the U.S. dollar.

It's best to carry traveler's checks and credit cards, plus cash when traveling. Traveler's checks are widely accepted. Many small restaurants, gasoline stations, and shops outside large urban areas will not accept bills over 20 dollars.

There are no restrictions on bringing in or taking out either Canadian or foreign currency. Your national currency, as well as traveler's checks, may be exchanged at most banks or at the airport. Try not to exchange currency at hotels or restaurants as they usually have less favorable exchange rates and include a surcharge. To obtain the best rate of exchange, first track currency fluctuations in the newspaper, and then change your money at a bank.

Business Hours and Closings. Banking hours are Monday through Friday from 10:00 A.M. until 3:00–6:00 P.M., depending upon the individual bank. Government offices and businesses are open from 9:00 A.M. to 5:00 P.M., Monday throught Friday. Department and retail stores are open Monday to Saturday, 10:00 A.M. until 6:00 or 7:00 P.M.; shopping malls are open 10:00 A.M. to 9:00 P.M. Monday through Friday, 10:00 A.M. to 6:00 P.M. on Saturday, and noon to 6:00 P.M. on Sunday. Some convenience and drug stores, as well as assorted fast-food establishments, are open 24 hours a day, seven days a week.

Museums are customarily open from 10:00 A.M. to 5:00 P.M. Tuesday through Friday; on weekends, they frequently do not open until noon. On Mondays, many museums, particularly the smaller ones, are closed. It is always best to check opening times by telephone before visiting a museum.

Postage. Post offices in cities and major towns are open Monday through Friday, 8:30 A.M. to 4:30 P.M. Stamps may be purchased in post offices, hotels, railroad stations, airports, and from vending machines in many small shops. Mail sent within the United States costs 25¢ an ounce, including postcards. Air mail to Europe and most destinations outside the United States, costs 50¢ an ounce. Other services available in post offices include express mail service and overnight mail.

Telephones. The area code for the entire state of Alaska is 907.

Local and long distance calls may be made from any of the public coin-operated telephones. Local calls cost 25¢ for the first five minutes, and an additional 25¢ for every subsequent five minutes. (Most phones accept any combination of change, excluding pennies.) For a long distance call, dial the area code and number first and the operator will instruct you to deposit the necessary coinage. In public areas, such as airports and train stations, there are phones that allow you to charge your call to your credit card call number.

Calls to other countries frequently have to go through the overseas operator (dial 0 for assistance). You can telephone direct to countries outside the U.S. by dialing the national code (for example, 011 44 for England) followed by the area code and the subscriber's number.

Help and emergency numbers in Alaska:

Emergency, police, fire	911
Local information	411
Operator	0
Alaska State Troopers info.	452-2114
Road Conditions	456-7623
Time/temperature	844
National Weather Service	456-0247
Statewide weather info.	456-0389

Traveling in Alaska. Despite its daunting size, Alaska has a profusion of transportation alternatives that make even the farthest reaches accessible.

Air Travel. Intra-state air travel, which includes air taxis, air charter services, and bush planes, provides immediate access to Alaska's remote towns and wilderness areas, and is the quickest way of traversing the huge state. Among the airlines that shuttle between the major cities are Air Pacific, Alaska Airlines, Delta Airlines, ERA Aviation, Hawaiian Air, Mark Air, Northwest Orient Airlines, Reeve Aleutian Airways, Ryan Air Service, Southcentral Air, and United Airlines.

If you are planning to make an extensive trek through secluded territory, hire a bush plane. Although expensive, there are distinct advantages to choosing this method of travel. For example, you can hire one for a "flightseeing" tour—a combination of flying and sightseeing—to see Alaska's spectacular, untouched scenery. If you are going camping in a remote area, you can arrange for your pilot to drop you off and then return to pick you up at a pre-arranged spot.

Buses. Most of Alaska is not accessible by bus; however, there are bus companies that offer wonderful package tours of Alaska. One of the most popular is the Gray Line of Alaska tours, which offers combined flight/rail/bus travel packages to places such as the immense Columbia Glacier, Sitka, and Denali National Park. Reservations may be made through Gray Line of Alaska, 547 West 4th Avenue, Anchorage, AK 99501, tel. (907) 277-5581 or 300 Elliott Avenue, West, Seattle, WA 98119, tel. (800) 445-2206. Other bus lines that offer comprehensive tour packages include Alaska-Denali Transit, Alaska Yukon Motorcoaches, Atlas Tours Ltd., Norline Coaches, Royal Highway Tours, Seward Bus Lines, Valdez/Anchorage Bus Lines, and White Pass and Yukon Motorcoaches.

Trains. The Alaska Railroad runs on specific, limited routes (mostly through southcentral Alaska), and reservations are required. During the summer, the Alaska Railroad system offers a daily connecting ride between Anchorage, Fairbanks, and Denali National Park. A marvelous alternative to flightseeing, train travel lets you relax in high-domed cars that offer great views of the beautiful Alaskan scenery, while covering long distances. You can receive additional information and make reservations through the Alaska Railroad, P.O. Box 107500, Anchorage, AK 99510, tel. (907) 265-2494 or (800) 544-0552.

Ferries. Alaska's extensive Marine Highway System consists of two separate state-run networks that interweave throughout the southeastern coastal (or Panhandle) region and the southwestern coastal region of Alaska.

The Marine Highway System cruises the Inside Passage past ice-blue glaciers, lovely cloistered islands, and countless bays and coves, permitting you to see some of the most amazing wildlife and sea life activity in Alaska. It links Hyder, Ketchikan, Wrangell, Petersburg, Sitka, Juneau, Haines, and Skagway. The southwestern network of the system threads its way from Seldovia to Homer, Seward, Whittier, Cordova, Valdez, and Kodiak.

You can also enter Alaska via the British Columbia ferry system, which provides transportation from Vancouver Island and Prince Rupert, B.C., where you can catch a connecting ferry on the Alaska Marine Highway's southeastern ferry system. For reservations, contact the British Columbia Ferry Corporation at either 1112 Fort Street, Victoria, B.C., Canada V8V 4V2, tel. (604) 386-3431; or 818 Braughton Street, Victoria, B.C., Canada V8W 1E4 (604) 669-1211.

Off-season fares, in effect from October to April, are 50 percent less; children under six years of age travel free; and children ages 6 to 11 travel for half fare. Senior citizens can travel free on the ferry systems from October 1 to May 15. You can also arrange to transport your car on the ferry. For reservations, contact the Alaska Marine Highway, Pouch R, Juneau, AK 99811, tel. (907) 456-3941 or (907) 272-7116. You must make complete reservations and render full payment at least 45 days before you intend to sail.

Driving in Alaska. Although operating a vehicle in Alaska may have its challenging moments due to the capricious weather and precarious road conditions, it is probably the easiest way to travel if you are planning to visit the national parks and camp. Renting a car may prove to be the wisest decision if you want to save wear and tear on your own car as Alaska's roadways contain some sour surprises, such as flying gravel and very uneven road surfaces. (This latter problem is usually caused by permafrost which causes the ground to heave and shift.) You must also watch out for any wildlife that might meander onto the road, including black bears, Dall sheep, and moose. If you do encounter an animal, stop the car and wait until it crosses. Do not get out of the car; if the animal does not move, honk your horn.

Only about one-third of Alaska's roadways are paved; gravel roads are more the norm, although even these may be scarce in some towns. Suppress any desire to speed, as gravel often causes vehicles to skid at high speeds.

The majority of Alaska's 15,315 miles (24,504 km.) of highways stretch across the Interior and Southcentral regions; they are well-traveled and frequently patrolled. However, it is always possible that you could be marooned somewhere, and this could translate into serious trouble if you've neglected to address some basic rules for traveling in Alaska. Pack a "doctor's bag" for your car which should include everything from anti-freeze, spark plugs, and fan belts to a spare flashlight, spare tires, and flares. It is crucial to travel with a full gas tank and carry a spare container to avoid being stranded on the road. Gas stations appear sporadically along the highways, especially in less densely populated regions, and they frequently shut down on holidays. Other items to pack include a sleeping bag, spare outer clothing for each person, and non-perishable, high-energy food, such as nuts or dried fruit. Plastic headlight shields are also a good precautionary purchase, especially in winter. Head off problems by checking your car before you leave any destination, and prevent accidents by stopping frequently to rest during each leg of your journey. During the wintertime, it is important to test your brakes frequently and be aware of icy patches on the roadway.

Documentation. If you are not a U.S. resident, international driver's licenses are valid in Alaska. Taking out temporary insurance is always sensible, especially due to less-than-optimum road conditions. If you do any driving in Canada in conjunction with your trip, you must obtain a Canadian Non-Resident Inter-Provincial Motor Vehicle Liability Insurance Card (you must have proof of $200,000 in third party automobile insurance in Canada), which protects you in the event of an accident.

Car Rentals. You can find car rental agencies in every major city in Alaska, and frequently in smaller towns. Companies include A-1 Auto Rental, Alamo, Avis, Budget, Hertz, National, Payless, and Thrifty. Other companies, such as Rent-A-Dent and Rent-A-Heap, lease slightly damaged cars at discount prices. Call ahead for price quotes as well as restrictions; some agencies object to their cars being driven on rough roads like the gravelly Dalton Highway, Denali Highway, Elliott Highway, Steese Highway, or Taylor Highway.

Driving Regulations. As it is throughout the United States, driving is on the right hand side of the road. At an intersection, the car on the right always has the right of way. A right turn at a red light is permitted unless otherwise indicated.

Gasoline. Hours at gas stations vary due to the season and weather. While many gas stations are closed on Sundays and holidays in smaller towns, there are 24-hour stations open every day on major highways at approximately every 20 to 50 miles (32 to 82 km.). Gasoline is sold by the gallon, and is available in super unleaded, unleaded, regular, and diesel. Fuel prices tend to be high, despite the presence of the pipeline. Credit cards are accepted at many stations, although cash is always your best bet.

Speed limits. The speed limit on major highways is 55 m.p.h. (90 km.), 40 m.p.h. (65 km.) on side roads, 30 m.p.h. (50 km.) in cities and towns, and 20 m.p.h. (30 km.) in areas such as school zones.

Traffic accidents and road assistance. Dial 911 or 0 for the operator in any emergency and you will be put through to the police or fire department, or given directory assistance. If you are a member of the Automobile Association of America (AAA), you can dial their toll-free number, 1-800-336-HELP, and they will give you a local number to call for towing assistance. AAA provides road maps and general information to its members about road and weather conditions. State troopers constantly patrol the highways, offering aid to stranded motorists. In the case of a breakdown or an accident, you can call them at (907) 789-2161.

Tour Operators. A number of tour operators offer specialized tour packages to Alaska that concentrate on particular interests, such as sightseeing, camping, kayaking, hiking, bicycling, or nature-watching. While many tours are pre-packaged, they usually offer enough flexibility for travelers to go off on their own and then rejoin the tour. Other tour operators will be happy to assist you in customizing your own itinerary. The following is a list of the major tour operators for Alaska.

Alaska Association of Mountain
Wilderness Guides
Box 3685
Anchorage, AK 99510
tel. (907) 276-6634

AlaskaBound
320 West Dock St.
Ketchikan, AK 99901
tel. (800) 544-0808

Alaska Denali Guiding
Box 326
Talkeetna, AK 99676
tel. (907) 733-2649

Alaska Discovery
418 South Franklin St.
Juneau, AK 99802
tel. (907) 586-3822

Alaska River Adventures
1831 Kuskokwim St.
Anchorage, AK 99521
tel. (907) 276-3418

Alaska Travel Adventures
200 North Franklin St.
Juneau, AK 99801
tel. (907) 586-6245

Gray Line of Alaska
547 West 4th Ave.
Anchorage, AK 99501
tel. (907) 277-5581

Midnight Sun Tours
Box 103355
Anchorage, AK 99510
tel. (907) 276-8687

Outdoor Alaska
Box 7814
Ketchikan, AK 99901
tel. (907) 247-8444

TravAlaska Tours
349 Wrangell Ave.
Anchorage, AK 99501
tel. (907) 276-1305

Tour Alaska
2555 76th Ave., S.E.
Mercer Island, WA 98040
tel. (800) 835-8907

Camping and Wilderness Exploration. Camping and hiking are certainly the finest ways to experience Alaska's unsurpassed beauty up close. National and state parks abound in Alaska, and offer a variety of inexpensive facilities. Most campgrounds are open from late May through September; although you cannot make reservations, you can guarantee a campsite by choosing an area early in the day and setting up your tent. Amenities vary at each site; some offer simple toilet facilities and supplies of firewood, while others provide only a water pump. Since firewood is usually in scant supply at most campgrounds, you might consider packing a small stove to ensure a hot meal. (If you do build a fire, always bank it to keep the flame steady and low, and be certain that it is completely extinguished before you continue on your way.) For a listing of state facilities, parks and campgrounds, as well as general information on camping regulations, contact the Alaska State Division of Outdoor Recreation and Parks, Box 10-7001, Anchorage, AK 99510; tel. (907) 762-4565.

Bears. When walking in an area likely to have bears, make plenty of noise: Bears have poor eyesight but they have very good hearing and since they are normally shy of humans, they'll avoid them if possible. Try tying a bell to your bag, or rattling stones in a tin cup. Take the following precautions: *Never* keep food in your tent and never leave leftovers at a campsite; keep it wrapped up in airtight bags in your car or hang it in a tree at least 12 feet (3.5 meters) from the ground. Wash your cooking utensils and dishes immediately after use, as the odor might attract animals. *Never* try to feed or touch a bear, however tame it may seem. If you do suddenly encounter a bear, retreat slowly, facing the animal; do not panic and run, or the bear will run after you. Another option that sounds pretty risky to us is to drop to the ground and play dead; we're told that the bear may sniff at you, but he will eventually leave you alone.

Equipment and Precautions. It is wise to carry emergency equipment whether you go on an extended wilderness jaunt or a day-long hike; basic items to include are a compass, maps, a first aid kit, insect repellent, waterproof matches, and a multipurpose utensil such as a Swiss army knife.

For a trip lasting more than a day, you should pack the following items:

a sleeping bag with fiberfill (down feathers clump up when it rains), a tent equipped with a fine-mesh mosquito net, cooking utensils, flares or distress signals, and a shovel.

During the summer, a potent insect repellent, such as Off or Cutter, is indispensable; without it, you could become a tasty meal for thousands of insects and bugs. In addition to applying repellent to exposed skin, also spray your clothes and sleeping bag (mosquitoes, midges, and no-see-ums can sting through tightly fit clothing).

Pack clothing appropriate to Alaska's changeable climate; the key to staying warm is to dress in layers. Layers of clothing provide extra insulation and can be easily removed if you get too warm. This practice prevents hypothermia, a very real threat in this climate. Thermal underwear is essential after sundown, and fiberfill parkas or heavy lumber jackets make for warm, comfortable outerwear. For hiking and climbing, sturdy waterproof hiking boots are a must. If you are traveling into the high precipitation regions, remember to pack insulated rain boots for the likely downpour, as well as general rain gear (forget the umbrella and wear a rain slicker with a hood instead). Woolen socks, gloves, and a hat are smart to bring with you.

While nature may tempt you to drink directly from a clear, rushing stream, you should remember that many bodies of water are infected by a parasite called giardia lamblia. It can cause intense weakness, abdominal cramping, and general nausea. To prevent ingesting this parasite, purify the water by boiling it for a full five minutes before you drink it.

Forest rangers are always concerned about the welfare of visitors, even when they intend to stay close to their campsite. Before setting out on a hike, you should report to the park ranger and leave a detailed map of your intended route, plus approximate dates of your stay. When you return, check in again with the rangers so they won't consider you missing and start a search for you.

Sports. If one of your objectives is to test your sports skills, or develop new ones, Alaska will meet that challenge with the bounty of its land and waters. It is easily understandable why Alaskans and visitors alike spend most of their time out of doors. Consider the opportunities for kayaking, dog-sledding, downhill skiing, fishing, backpacking, hunting, white-water rafting, ice fishing, and hot air ballooning, and you've just scratched the surface of possibilities for outdoor activities around Alaska.

Alaska is a veritable cornucopia of fish and wildlife; seasoned hunters and anglers and novice sportsmen alike will revel in the pursuit of their hobby in paradisiac surroundings. If you are a die-hard sportsman, fishing and hunting packages are available through wilderness lodges; albeit costly, they permit you to spend concentrated amounts of time on your sport in more cloistered areas of the wilderness.

The extraordinary size and supply of fish here is dumbfounding.

Salmon lovers will reap tremendous rewards in Alaska, where five varieties crowd its waters—chum, red, silver, pink, and king. Major salmon collectives are located in Anchorage, Cordova, the Copper River Basin, Kodiak, Nome, Seward, Skagway, and Valdez. Other species that ply Alaska's waters include arctic char, rainbow trout, grayling, shrimp, crabs, flounder, halibut, sea bass, and red snapper. Contact the Alaska Department of Fish and Game (see below) for permits and to find out the seasons for the types of fish you're interested in catching.

Hunters will undoubtedly find satisfaction in the wide variety of game from which to choose, including black and brown/grizzly bears, mountain goats, moose, dall sheep, ptarmigan, black-tailed deer, ducks, and geese. Hunting is prohibited in the national parks. You must purchase a hunting license and game tags, available through the Alaska Department of Fish and Game (see below), if you intend to hunt large game. The office also issues information on hunting regulations and seasonal shooting restrictions. Foreign visitors tracking big game, such as brown/grizzly bear, moose, or musk ox, must be accompanied on expeditions by a guide.

Fishing gear and sporting guns may be taken into the state, but guns and ammunition need to be registered at customs. Non-resident anglers must purchase a fishing permit, available through the Alaska Department of Fish and Game, Box 3-2000, Juneau, AK 99802.

National Parks and Wilderness Refuges. Although not exhaustive, we have compiled a listing of many of Alaska's state and national parks and wilderness refuge centers. If you wish, you can contact them to receive listings of campsites and facilities in their areas, as well as information on hiking, kayaking, nature walks and other expeditions they sponsor.

State and National Parks

Alaska State Parks
400 Willoughby Ave.
Juneau, AK 99801
tel. (907) 465-4563

Alaska Division of Parks and
  Outdoor Recreation
Southcentral Regional Pouch 7001
Anchorage, AK 99510
tel. (907) 561-2020

Superintendent
Gates of the Arctic National Park
  and Preserve
P.O. Box 74680
Fairbanks, AK 99707
tel. (907) 456-0281

Chugach National Forest
201 East 9th Ave., Suite 206
Anchorage, AK 99501
tel. (907) 271-2500

Chugach State Park
Pouch 7001
Anchorage, AK 99510
tel. (907) 561-2020

USDA Forest Service
Cordova Office, P.O. Box 280
Cordova, AK 99574
tel. (907) 424-7661

Superintendent
Denali National Park and Preserve
P.O. Box 9
McKinley Park, AK 99755
tel. (907) 683-2294

Division of Parks and Outdoor
   Recreation
P.O. Box 107001
Anchorage, AK 99510
tel. (907) 561-2020

Division of Parks and Outdoor
   Recreation
Northern Regional Manager
4418 Airport Way
Fairbanks, AK 99709
tel. (907) 456-4218

Superintendent
Glacier Bay National Park and
   Preserve
Gustavus, AK 99826
tel. (907) 697-2230

Superintendent
Katmai National Park and Preserve
P.O. Box 7
King Salmon, AK 99613
tel. (907) 246-3305

Kenai District
Division of Parks and Outdoor
Recreation
P.O. Box 1247
Soldotna, AK 99669
tel. (907) 561-2020

Kenai Fjords National Park
P.O. Box 1727
Seward, AK 99664
tel. (907) 224-3175

Kobuk Valley National Park
P.O. Box 1029
Kotzebue, AK 99752
tel. (907) 442-3890

Division of Parks and Outdoor
   Recreation
Kodiak District
S.R. Box 3800
Kodiak, AK 99615
tel. (907) 486- 6339

Superintendent
Klondike Gold Rush National
   Historical Park
P.O. Box 517
Skagway, AK 99840
tel. (907) 983-2921

Lake Clark National Park and
   Preserve
701 C St., Box 61
Anchorage, AK 99513
tel. (907) 271- 3751

Alaska State Parks
Mat-Su District Office
P.O. Box 182
Palmer, AK 99645
tel. (907) 745-3975

USDA Forest Service
Seward Office, P.O. Box 390
Seward, AK 99664

Tongass National Forest
Regional Office, P.O. Box 21628,
   PAO
Juneau, AK 99802
tel. (907) 586-8806

Tongass National Forest
Chatham Area
204 Siginaka Way
Sitka, AK 99835
tel. (907) 747- 6671

Tongass National Forest
Stikine Area
P.O. Box 309
Petersburg, AK 99833
tel. (907) 772-3841

Wrangell-St. Elias National Park
  and Preserve
P.O. Box 29
Glennallen, AK 99588
tel. (907) 822- 5235

Yukon-Charley Rivers National
  Preserve
P.O. Box 64
Eagle, AK 99738
tel. (907) 547-2233

Wildlife Refuges

Refuge Manager
Alaska Maritime National Wildlife
  Refuge
202 Pioneer Ave.
Homer, AK 99603
tel. (907) 235-6546

Refuge Manager
Alaska Peninsula/Becharof
  National Wildlife Refuge
P.O. Box 277
King Salmon, AK 99613
tel. (907) 246-3339

Regional Manager
Arctic National Wildlife Refuge,
  Rm. 266
Federal Building and Courthouse
101 12th Ave., Box 20
Fairbanks, AK 99701
tel. (907) 456-0250

Superintendent
Bering Land Bridge National
  Preserve
P.O. Box 220
Nome, AK 99762
tel. (907) 443-2522

Alaska Division of Natural
  Resources
Division of Parks and Outdoor
  Recreation
Chugach/Southwest Area
P.O Box 107001
Anchorage, AK 99510
tel. (907) 694-9254

Innoko National Wildlife Refuge
P.O. Box 69
McGrath, AK 99627
tel. (907) 524-3251

Izembek National Wildlife Refuge
P.O. Box 127
Cold Bay, AK 99571
tel. (907) 532-2445

Regional Manager
Kanuti National Wildlife Refuge
Federal Building and Courthouse
P.O. Box 20
Fairbanks, AK 99701
tel. (907) 456-0329

Refuge Manager
Kenai National Wildlife Refuge
P.O. Box 2139
Soldotna, AK 99669
tel. (907) 262-7021

Refuge Manager
Kodiak National Wildlife Refuge
1390 Buskin River Rd.
Kodiak, AK 99615
tel. (907) 487-2600

Regional Manager
Koyukuk National Wildlife Refuge
P.O. Box 287
Galena, AK 99741
tel. (907) 656-1231

Regional Manager
Nowitna National Wildlife Refuge
P.O. Box 287
Galena, AK 99741
tel. (907) 656-1231

Regional Manager
Selawik National Wildlife Refuge
P.O. Box 270
Kotzebue, AK 99752
tel. (907) 442-3799

Refuge Manager
Tetlin National Wildlife Refuge
P.O. Box 155
Tok, AK 99780
tel. (907) 883-5312

Regional Manager
Tongiak National Wildlife Refuge
P.O. Box 270
Dillingham, AK 99576
tel. (907) 842-1063

Regional Manager
Yukon Delta National Wildlife
    Refuge
P.O. Box 346
Bethel, AK 99559
tel. (907) 543-3151

Regional Manager
Yukon Flats National Wildlife
    Refuge Federal Building and
    Courthouse
P.O. Box 20
Fairbanks, AK 99701
tel. (907) 456-0440

Shopping. No doubt you will want to carry away some memento of your trip to Alaska, and you can be sure there are wonderfully unique goods to be found here. Alaska's native handicrafts will tempt you with their distinctive beauty and designs. Items that are manufactured in Alaska carry the "Made in Alaska" logo of a polar bear and cub. Articles that are actually hand-crafted in Alaska bear the "Authentic Handicraft from Alaska" logo with a silhouette of the state or the "Authentic Native Handicraft from Alaska" logo with the silhouette of a hand.

The annual winter Anchorage Fur Rendezvous boasts the world's biggest fur auction; however, you can purchase fur products fashioned from beaver, mink, seal, reindeer, wolf, fox, caribou, and squirrel pelts year-round. You'll find exquisitely crafted coats, fur-lined parkas, mittens, and hats at reasonable prices throughout Alaska. Qivuit, the fur of the musk ox bred in Unalakleet, is woven into warm and beautiful outer garments.

Charm bracelets, earrings, necklaces, and other trinkets are wrought from gold. Delicate jewelry and figurines carved from ivory, hematite, and jade are among the state's specialties, as is ivory painstakingly etched with scrimshaw work. The Athapaskan Indians fashion jewelry and create other decorative items with beads that are deftly sewn into vibrant patterns.

Traditional Eskimo articles for sale include naturally insulated seal or reindeer skin boots (called mukluks) and ulus, which are unusual, fan-shaped knives designed for skinning and cutting tough hides. The Tlingit, Tsimshian, and Haida Indians carve extraordinary totem poles, as well as cunning masks. Aleutian baskets are woven from diverse materials, including birch bark and baleen, a substance collected from the upper jaw of bowhead whales.

Alaska also offers unusual edible treats. Reindeer meat and salmon can be salted, smoked, packaged, and sent to your home. So-called squaw candy, another typically Alaskan food, is salmon that has been smoked until it is very chewy and tasty.

Clothing Sizes. Listed below are standard clothing size equivalents for the United States, Great Britain, and Europe:

		U.S.	U.K.	Europe
Chest	Small	34	34	87
	Medium	36	36	91
		38	38	97
	Large	40	40	102
		42	42	107
	Extra Large	44	44	112
		46	46	117
Collar		14	14	36
		14$\frac{1}{2}$	14$\frac{1}{2}$	37
		15	15	38
		15$\frac{1}{2}$	15$\frac{1}{2}$	39
		16	16	41
		16$\frac{1}{2}$	16$\frac{1}{2}$	42
		17	17	43
Waist		24	24	61
		26	26	66
		28	28	71
		30	30	76
		32	32	80
		34	34	87
		36	36	91
		38	38	97

	U.S.	**U.K.**	**Europe**
Men's Suits	34	34	44
	35	35	46
	36	36	48
	37	37	49$\frac{1}{2}$
	38	38	51
	39	39	52$\frac{1}{2}$
	40	40	54
	41	41	55$\frac{1}{2}$
	42	42	57
Men's Shoes	7	6	39$\frac{1}{2}$
	8	7	41
	9	8	42
	10	9	43
	11	10	44$\frac{1}{2}$
	12	11	46
	13	12	47
Men's Hats	6$\frac{3}{4}$	6$\frac{5}{8}$	54
	6$\frac{7}{8}$	6$\frac{3}{4}$	55
	7	6$\frac{7}{8}$	56
	7$\frac{1}{8}$	7	57
	7$\frac{1}{4}$	7$\frac{1}{8}$	58
	7$\frac{1}{2}$	7$\frac{3}{8}$	60
Women's Dresses	6	8	36
	8	10	38
	10	12	40
	12	14	42
	14	16	44
	16	18	46
	18	20	48
Women's Blouses and Sweaters	8	10	38
	10	12	40
	12	14	42
	14	16	44
	16	18	46
	18	20	48
Women's Shoes	4$\frac{1}{2}$	3	35$\frac{1}{2}$
	5	3$\frac{1}{2}$	36
	5$\frac{1}{2}$	4	36$\frac{1}{2}$
	6	4$\frac{1}{2}$	37
	6$\frac{1}{2}$	5	37$\frac{1}{2}$
	7	5$\frac{1}{2}$	38
	7$\frac{1}{2}$	6	38$\frac{1}{2}$
	8	6$\frac{1}{2}$	39
	8$\frac{1}{2}$	7	39$\frac{1}{2}$
	9	7$\frac{1}{2}$	40
Children's Clothing	2	16	92
(*One size larger for knitwear*)	3	18	98

Clothing Sizes (cont'd)

	U.S.	U.K.	Europe
	4	20	104
	5	22	110
	6	24	116
	6X	26	122
Children's Shoes	8	7	24
	9	8	25
	10	9	27
	11	10	28
	12	11	29
	13	12	30
	1	13	32
	2	1	33
	3	2	34
	4½	3	36
	5½	4	37
	6½	5½	38½

General Sources of Information. Below is a listing of information sources in Alaska. They provide travel assistance, including maps, and hotel and restaurant directories, as well as pamphlets on weekly and monthly events.

Alaska State Division of Tourism
P.O. Box E
Juneau, AK 99811
tel. (907) 465-2012

Alaska State Division of Tourism
3601 C St., Suite 722
Anchorage, AK 99811
tel. (907) 563-2167

Anchorage Convention and
    Visitors Bureau
201 East Third Ave.
Anchorage, AK 99501
tel. (907) 276-4118

Anchorage Log Cabin Visitors
    Information Center
F St. and Fourth Ave.
Anchorage, AK 99501
tel. (907) 274-3531

Fairbanks Visitors and
    Convention Bureau
550 First Ave.
Fairbanks, AK 99701
tel. (907) 456-5774

Haines Visitors Center
Second and Willard Sts.
Haines, AK 99827
tel. (907) 766-2202

Homer Convention and Visitors
    Bureau
P.O. Box 2706
Homer, AK 99603
tel. (907) 235-7875

Juneau Convention and Visitors
    Bureau
76 Egan Dr., Suite 140
Juneau, Alaska 99811
tel. (907) 586-1737

Kachekmak Bay Visitors and
  Convention Association
3776 Lake St.
Homer, AK 99603
tel. (907) 235-6030

Kenai Peninsula Convention and
  Visitors Bureau
P.O. Box 497
Kenai, AK 99611
tel. (907) 283-7989

Ketchikan Visitors Bureau
131 Front St.
Ketchikan, AK 99901
tel. (907) 225-6166

Kodiak Island Convention and
  Visitors Bureau
100 Marine Way
Kodiak, AK 99615
tel. (907) 486-4782

Mat-Su Convention and
  Visitors Bureau
P.O. Box 875747
Wasilla, AK 99687
tel. (907) 745-4840

Nome Convention and
  Visitors Bureau
P.O. Box 251
Nome, AK 99762
tel. (907) 443-5535

Sitka Visitors Bureau
P.O. Box 1226
Sitka, AK 99835
tel. (907) 747-5940

Skagway Convention and
  Visitors Bureau
P.O. Box 415
Skagway, AK 99840
tel. (907) 983-2854

Valdez Convention and
  Visitors Bureau
P.O. Box 1603
Valdez, AK 99686
tel. (907) 835-2984

Wrangell Visitors Bureau
P.O. Box 1078
Wrangell, AK 99929
tel. (907) 874-3770

TOWN-BY-TOWN

This section is organized alphabetically by town. Each listing provides information on tourist offices and ground transportation, including guided tour organizations, and accommodations. Hotels are classified according to our own rating system, which is based on the one used by the Alaska State Division of Tourism (see page 134 for a full explanation).

Anchorage
Information: Anchorage Convention and Visitors Bureau, 201 East Third Ave., tel. (907) 276-4118; Log Cabin Visitor Information Center, 4th Ave./F St., tel. (907) 274-3531 (open 7:30 A.M.–7:00 P.M. June–August; 8:30 A.M.–6:00 P.M. May and September, 9:00 A.M.–4:00 P.M.

the rest of the year); tel. for daily calendar events, (907) 276-3200. **Transportation:** *Air:* International Airport, 6.5 miles (10.5 km.) southwest. *Train:* Alaska Railroad (to Denali National Park, Fairbanks, Seward, and Whittier); tel. (800) 544-0552. *Bus:* (to Arctic, southcentral, southeastern Alaska, and western Canada). *Car:* Take the Glenn Hwy. southwest directly to Anchorage, or travel north via Sterling Hwy. *Tours:* Gray Line, tel. (907) 277-5581 (conducted tours to Barrow, Kodiak, southeastern Alaska, etc.; excursion in glass railway train to Denali National Park and Fairbanks). *City bus:* People Mover Mass Transit System, running Monday–Friday, 5:30 A.M.–11:00 P.M., Saturday 7:30 A.M.– 11:00 P.M., tel. (907) 264-6526. **Accommodations:** 🏠🏠🏠 (*Luxury*) Anchorage Hilton, 500 West 3rd Ave., tel. (907) 272-7411; Captain Cook Hotel, 5th Ave./K St., tel. (907) 276-6000. 🏠🏠🏠 Days Inn, 321 5th Ave., tel. (800) 325-2525. 🏠🏠 Anchorage Hotel, 330 E St., tel. (907) 272-4553; Super 8 Motel, 3501 Minnesota Dr., tel. (800) 843-1991. *Bed and Breakfast:* Alaska Private Lodgings, 1236 West 10th Ave., tel. (907) 258-1717; Bed and Breakfast Inn, 934 West Eighth Ave., tel. (907) 276-1901. *Hostels:* Anchorage International Hostel, 700 H St., tel. (907) 276-3635.

Angoon

Information: U.S. Forest Service's Admiralty Island National Monument office, tel. (907) 788-3166, or City Hall, tel. (907) 788-3653. **Transportation:** *Air:* Scheduled seaplane service from Juneau; Angoon private aircraft base one mile (1.5 km.) southeast. *Ferry:* Alaska Marine Highway System (southeastern route to ports including Skagway, Haines, Juneau/Auke Bay, Hoonah, Tenakee, Sitka, Kake, Petersburg, Wrangell, Hollis, Ketchikan, Metlakatla, Prince Rupert, B.C., and Seattle, WA), tel. (800) 642-0066. **Accommodations:** 🏠 Kootznahoo Inlet Lodge, tel. (907) 788-3501; Whalers Cove Lodge, tel. (907) 788-3123. *Bed and Breakfast:* Favorite Bay Inn, tel. (907) 788-3123.

Barrow

Information: Barrow Convention and Visitors Association, tel. (907) 852-8687. **Transportation:** *Air:* Service from Anchorage via Fairbanks; also air taxi service. **Accommodations:** 🏠🏠🏠 Barrow Airport Inn, P.O. Box 933, tel. 852-2525; Top of the World Hotel, P.O. Box 189, tel. 852-3900.

Bethel

Information: Bethel Chamber of Commerce, tel. (907) 543-2911. **Transportation:** *Air:* Scheduled service from Anchorage. **Accommodations:** 🏠🏠 Kuskokwim Inn, Box 888, tel. (907) 543-2207. 🏠 Bethel Inn, 454 Ptarmigan St., tel. (907) 543-3204.

Big Lake

Information: Matanuska-Susitna Convention and Visitors Bureau, tel. (907) 745-4840. **Transportation:** *Air:* Scheduled 15 minute flight from Anchorage. *Car:* Take George Parks Hwy. south to Big Lake Rd.; 6.5 miles (10.5 km.) to Big Lake. *Tours:* Islander and Big Lake Tours, tel. (907) 892-7144. **Accommodations:** 🏨 Klondike Inn, Lake Front Hotel, Box 521020, tel. (907) 892-6261. 🏨 Big Lake Motel, P.O. Box 520728, tel. (907) 892-7976. *Bed and Breakfast:* The Country Inn, tel. (907) 892-6312.

Cordova

Information: Cordova Chamber of Commerce, 1st St., tel. (907) 424-7260. **Transportation:** *Air:* Scheduled service from Anchorage. *Ferry:* Alaska Marine Highway System's southwestern route, connecting Cordova, Valdez, Whittier, Seward, Homer, Seldovia, Kodiak, and Port Lions. **Accommodations:** 🏨 Prince William Motel, P.O. Box 848, tel. (907) 424-3201; Reluctant Fisherman Inn, Box 150, tel. (907) 424-3272.

Craig

Information: Craig City Hall, open Monday–Friday, 8:00 A.M.– 5:00 P.M., tel. (907) 826-3275. **Transportation:** *Air:* Taxi service from Ketchikan. *Ferry:* Service from Ketchikan to terminal at Hollis; from there, travel by car to Craig. *Boat:* Charter boat service. **Accommodations:** 🏨 Haidaway Lodge, tel. (907) 826-3268; Ruth Ann's, tel. (907) 826-3377.

Delta Junction

Information: At junction of Alaska and Richardson hwys.; open June–September, 9:00 A.M.–6:00 P.M., tel. (907) 895-4600. **Transportation:** *Air:* Scheduled service going from Tok to Fairbanks, makes stop at Delta Junction. *Bus:* Alaska Yukon Motorcoaches. *Car:* Access via Alaska Hwy. **Accommodations:** 🏨 Alaska 6 Motel, Box 1115, tel. (907) 895-4848; Kelly's Motel, Box 8214, tel. (907) 895-4667; Trophy Lodge, Alaska Hwy., Mile 1,420.3, tel. (907) 895-4685. *Hostel:* Delta International Hostel, P.O. Box 971, tel. (907) 895-4627 or (907) 897-8002.

Denali National Park

Information: Denali National Park and Preserve, P.O. Box 9, Denali Park, tel. (907) 683-2297; National Park Service information center, 2525 Gambell St., Room 107, Anchorage, AK 99503, tel. (907) 271-2643. **Transportation:** *Air:* Scheduled service from Anchorage and Fairbanks; charter flights/flightseeing tours of park available. *Bus:* Daily summer bus service from Anchorage to Fairbanks, plus bus tours.

Shuttle bus service between Riley Creek information center and Wonder Lake. *Car:* Accessible from George Parks Hwy. and Denali Hwy. *Train:* Alaska Railroad runs between Anchorage and Fairbanks from May–September—stops at Denali National Park. Private, high-domed car called Midnight Sun Express also available as part of express train rides. *Boat trips:* Denali Raft Adventures, tel. (907) 683-2234 (summer) or (907) 337-9604 (winter); McKinley Raft Tours (raft trips on Nenana River), tel. (907) 683-2392. **Accommodations:** 🏠🏠🏠 *(Luxury)* Camp Denali (wilderness lodge), write to Box 67-TP, Denali National Park, tel. (907) 683-2290 (summer) or Box 216-TP, Cornish, New Hampshire, tel. (603) 675-2248 (winter); Denali National Park Hotel, tel. (907) 683-2215 (summer) or (907) 278-1122 (during winter, for spring reservations only); McKinley Chalet Resort, George Parks Hwy., Mile 239, tel. (907) 276-7234. 🏠🏠🏠 Harper Lodge at Denali, Parks Hwy., Mile 238.5, tel. (907) 683-2282; Mt. McKinley Village, Parks Hwy., Mile 224, tel. (907) 683-2265. 🏠🏠 Denali Crow's Nest Log Cabins, George Parks Hwy., Mile 238.5, tel. (907) 683-2723 or 683-2321; North Face Lodge, Box 67, tel. (907) 683-2290; Kantishna Roadhouse, tel. (907) 345-1160. *Bed and Breakfast:* McKinley/Denali Bed and Breakfast, tel. (907) 683-2258 or 683-2273; McKinley Wilderness Lodge, P.O. Box 63 M, tel. (907) 683-2277 (summer) or (907) 274-5366 (winter).

Dillingham

Transportation: *Air:* Scheduled service from Anchorage; charter service. **Accommodations:** 🏠🏠 The Bristol Inn, Box 71, tel. (907) 842-2240; The Dillingham Hotel, Box 194, tel. (907) 842-5316. 🏠 Ekwok Lodge (48 miles east of Dillingham), tel. (907) 842-1075.

Fairbanks

Information: Fairbanks Visitors and Convention Bureau, 550 1st Ave., tel. (907) 456-5774 (open daily in summer 8:30 A.M.–7:00 P.M.; 8:30 A.M.–5:00 P.M. Monday–Friday in winter); tel. for daily calendar of events, 456-INFO. **Transportation:** *Air:* International airport 6 miles (10 km.) east from downtown; charter flights. *Bus:* service to Anchorage and western Canada. *Tours:* Gold Rush Tours, tel. (907) 456-5414; Gray Line of Fairbanks, tel. (907) 456-7742. *City bus:* Metropolitan Area Commuter Service (MACS), running Monday–Friday, 6:45 A.M.–10:40 P.M.; tel. (907) 452-3279. *Boat trips:* riverboats *Discovery I* and *Discovery II* (cruise down Chena and Tanana rivers), write to Alaska Riverways, P.O. Box 80610, Fairbanks, AK 99708, tel. (907) 479-6673. *Train:* Alaska Railroad (to Anchorage, Denali National Park, Seward, and Whittier), tel. (800) 544-0552. **Accommodations:** 🏠🏠🏠 *(Luxury)* Westmark Fairbanks, 820 Noble St., tel. (800) 426-0327; Westmark Inn, 1521 South Cushman St., tel. (800) 426-0327. 🏠🏠🏠 Captain

Bartlett Inn, 1141 Airport Way, tel. (800) 544-7528; Regency Fairbanks, 95 Tenth Ave., tel. (907) 452-3200. 🏠 Traveler's Inn, 813 Noble St., tel. (907) 456-7722; Klondike Inn, 1316 Bedrock St., tel. (907) 479-6241; Alaska Motor Inn, 419 4th Ave., tel. (907) 456-5414. 🏠 Tamarac Inn Motel, 252 Minnie St., tel. 456-6406. *Hostels:* Fairbanks International Youth Hostel, P.O. Box 2196, tel. (907) 452-6928. *Bed and Breakfast:* Fairbanks Bed and Breakfast, Box 74573, tel. (907) 452-4967; Goldstream Bed and Breakfast, tel. (907) 455-6550.

Fort Yukon

Transportation: *Air:* Scheduled service from Fairbanks, available charter service. *Boat:* Charter service. **Accommodations:** 🏠 Gwitchyaa Zhee Lodge, Box 155, tel. (907) 662-2468; New Sourdough Hotel, P.O. Box 109, tel. (907) 662-2402.

Glacier Bay National Park/Gustavus

Information: Superintendent, Glacier Bay National Park, Gustavus, AK 99826, tel. (907) 697-2230. **Transportation:** *Air:* Scheduled service from Juneau; charter flights also from Juneau, Skagway, Sitka, and Haines. *Boat:* Glacier Express (catamaran—leaves from downtown Juneau, June–August), contact Glacier Bay Yacht Tours, 76 Egan Dr., Suite 110, Juneau, AK 99801, tel. (907) 586-6835; excursion tour boats from Bartlett Cove to Glacier Bay. *Tours:* Gustavus Inn Charters, Box 31, tel. (907) 586-2006 (winter); tel. (907) 697-2255 (*summer*). *Bus:* Shuttle bus available between Gustavus airport and Bartlett Cove. **Accommodations:** 🏠 Glacier Bay Lodge, P.O. Box 108, tel. (800) 622-2042 or (800) 697-2225. 🏠 Gustavus Inn, P.O. Box 31, tel. (907) 697-2254; Glacier Bay Country Inn, Box 5, tel. (907) 697-2288. *Bed and Breakfast:* The Puffin, Box 3-MP, tel. (907) 697-2260 (summer) or (907) 789-9787 (winter).

Glennallen

Transportation: *Bus:* Scheduled service between Valdez and Anchorage. *Car:* Located at south junction of Glenn and Richardson hwys. *Tours:* Alaska Wilderness Outfitters, Box 516, Glennallen, AK 99588. **Accommodations:** 🏠 Ahtna Lodge, Box 88, tel. (907) 822-3288 or 822-3289. 🏠 Caribou Motel, Box 329, tel. (907) 822-3302; Ranch House Lodge, Glenn Hwy., Mile 173, tel. (907) 822-3882.

Haines

Information: Haines Chamber of Commerce, Box 518, Haines, AK 99827, or the Visitors Center at 2nd and Willard Sts., daily summer hours from 8:00 A.M.–8:00 P.M., tel. (907) 766-2202. **Transportation:** *Air:* Charter flights. *Ferry:* Alaska Marine Highway System's southeastern route (ports include Anchorage, Skagway, Juneau/Auke Bay, Hoonah, Tenakee, Sitka, Kake, Petersburg, Wrangell, Hollis, Ketchikan, Metlakatla, Prince Rupert, B.C., and Seattle, WA), tel. (800) 642-0066. *Bus:* Local service. *Car:* Take Haines Hwy. directly to Haines. **Accommodations:** 🏨 Hotel Hälsingland, Box 1589, tel. (800) 542-6363 or (907) 766-2000; Captain's Choice Motel, Box 392, tel. (800) 247-7153 or (907) 766-3111. 🏠 Cache Inn Lodge, Box 1045, tel. (907) 766-2910; Eagle's Nest Motel, Box 250, tel. (907) 766-2352; Fort Seward Lodge, Box 307, tel. (907) 766-2009. *Hostels:* Beaver Creek Camp and Youth Hostel, Box 1158, tel. (907) 766-2259.

Homer

Information: Homer Convention and Visitors Bureau, P.O. Box 2706, tel. (907) 235-7875; Homer Chamber of Commerce, Box 541, tel. (907) 235-7740, open daily May–September, from 1:00–9:00 P.M. **Transportation:** *Air:* Scheduled service from Anchorage; charter services available. *Ferry:* Alaska Marine Highway System's southwestern route (ports include Cordova, Valdez, Whittier, Seward, Seldovia, Kodiak, and Port Lions), tel. (800) 642-0066. **Accommodations:** 🏨 Best Western Bidarka Inn, Sterling Hwy., Mile 172.5, tel. (907) 235-8148; Heritage Hotel, 147 East Pioneer Ave., tel. 235-7787. 🏠 Ocean Shores Motel, Sterling Hwy., Mile 172.6, tel. (907) 235-7775; Baycrest Motel, Sterling Hwy., Mile 170, tel. (907) 235-8716; Driftwood Inn, 135 West Bunnell Ave., tel (907) 235-8019. *Bed and Breakfast:* Magic Canyon Ranch, 40015 Waterman Rd., tel. (907) 235-6077; Homer Bed and Breakfast, Box 1264, tel. (907) 235-8996; Wild Rose Bed and Breakfast, 5010 East Hill Rd., tel. (907) 235-8780; Pioneer Bed and Breakfast, P.O. Box 3082, tel. (907) 235-5670.

Juneau

Information: Juneau Convention and Visitors Bureau, 76 Egan Dr., Suite 140, tel. (907) 586-1737; Davis Log Cabin Information Center, 134 3rd St., open Monday–Friday 8:30 A.M.–5:00 P.M., additional weekend hours during the summer, 10:00 A.M.–5:00 P.M., tel. (907) 586-2201 or 586-2284. For daily calendar of events, call 586-JUNO. Information kiosk located in Marine Park, open 9:00 A.M.–6:00 P.M., June–September. **Transportation:** *Air:* Juneau International Airport. *Ferry:* Alaska Marine Highway System's southeastern route includes Skagway, Haines, Anchorage, Hoonah, Tenakee, Sitka, Kake, Petersburg, Wrangell, Hollis, Metlakatla, Prince Rupert, B.C., and Seattle, WA, tel. (800) 642-0066. Frequent stop for cruise ships. *Bus:* Capital Transit System runs locally and to Auke Bay, Douglas, and Mendenhall Valley. *Car:* Glacier Hwy. leads directly to Juneau. *Tours:* Glacier Bay

Yacht Tours, tel. (907) 586-6835 (trips to Glacier Bay); Ward Air, tel. (907) 789-9150 (sightseeing flights). Other excursions go to destinations such as Admiralty Island and Mendenhall Glacier. **Accommodations:** 🏨🏨🏨 Prospector Hotel, 375 Whittier Ave., tel. (800) 331-2711 or (907) 586-3737; The Baranof Hotel, 127 North Franklin St., tel. (800) 344-0970 or (907) 586-2660; Westmark Juneau, 51 W. Egan Dr., tel. (800) 544-0970 or (907) 586-6900. 🏨🏨 Alaskan Hotel (historic hotel), 167 South Franklin St., tel. (907) 586-1000; The Breakwater, 1711 Glacier Ave., tel. (800) 544-2250 or (907) 586-6303. 🏨 Super 8 Motel, 2295 Trout St., tel. (800) 843-1991 or (907) 789-4858; Driftwood Lodge, 435 Willoughby Ave., tel. (907) 586-2280. *Bed and Breakfast:* Dawson's Bed and Breakfast, 1941 Glacier Hwy., tel. (907) 586-9708; Alaska Bed and Breakfast Association (reservation service for Juneau, Sitka, Skagway, Petersburg, Haines, Angoon, Gustavus, etc.), 127 South Franklin St., tel. (907) 586-2959; Windsock Inn Bed and Breakfast, Box 223, tel. (907) 364-2431. *Hostel:* Juneau International Hostel, 614 Harris St., tel. (907) 586-9559.

Kenai

Information: Kenai Peninsula Convention and Visitors Bureau, P.O. Box 497, tel. (907) 283-7989; Kenai Chamber of Commerce, 402 Overland St., in "Moosemeat" John Hedburg's cabin, open Monday–Friday, 9:00 A.M.–5:00 P.M., tel. (907) 283-7989. **Transportation:** *Air:* Charter service. *Bus:* Charter service. **Accommodations:** 🏨 Kenai Merit Inn, 260 South Willow St., tel. (800) 544-0970 or (907) 283-7566; King Oscar's Motel, Kenai Spur Rd. at Airport Way, tel. (907) 283-6060; Uptown Motel, 47 Spur View Dr., tel. (907) 283-3660. *Bed and Breakfast:* Daniels Lake Lodge Bed and Breakfast, P.O. Box 1444, tel. 776-5578.

Ketchikan

Information: Ketchikan Visitors Bureau, 131 Front St., open daily 9:00 A.M.–5:00 P.M., May–September, tel. (907) 225-6166. **Transportation:** *Air:* Ketchikan International Airport, located on Gravina Island. Ferry shuttle between airport and shore. Charter service also available. *Ferry:* Alaska Marine Highway System's southeastern route. Ketchikan also port of call for cruise ships. Charter boats available for guided tours and fishing/sightseeing trips. *Bus:* Charter service. **Accommodations:** 🏨🏨 Ingersoll Hotel (historic hotel), 303 Mission St., tel. (907) 225-2124; Gilmore Hotel, 326 Front St., tel. (907) 225-9423; Royal Executive Suites, 1471 Tongass Ave., tel. (907) 225-1900. 🏨 Super 8 Motel, Box 8818, tel. (800) 843-1991 or (907) 225-9088; The Landing, 3434 Tongass Ave., tel. (907) 225-5166. *Hostel:* Ketchikan Youth Hostel, First United Methodist Church, Grant and Main Sts., tel. (907) 225-3319.

King Salmon

Transportation: *Air:* Scheduled service from Anchorage. **Accommodations:** 🏨 Ponderosa Inn, P.O. Box 234, tel. (907) 246-3444; Quinnat Landing, Box 418, tel. (907) 246-3000. 🏨 King Ko Inn, tel. 346-3378.

Klawock

Transportation: *Air:* Charter service. *Boat:* Charter service. *Ferry:* Service to Hollis. **Accommodations:** 🏨 Fireweed Lodge, P.O. Box 116, tel. (907) 755-2930; 🏨 Prince of Wales Lodge.

Kodiak

Information: Kodiak Island Convention and Visitors Bureau and Kodiak Visitors Information Center, 100 Marine Way, open Monday–Friday, 8:00 A.M.–5:00 P.M., tel. (907) 486-4782 or 486-4070. **Transportation:** *Air:* Scheduled service from Anchorage. *Ferry:* Alaska Marine Highway System's southwestern route. *Tours:* Gray Line of Alaska, tel. (800) 544-2206 (island tours). **Accommodations:** 🏨🏨🏨 Westmark Kodiak, 236 South Rezanof Dr., tel. (800) 544-0970 or (907) 486-5712. 🏨🏨 Kodiak Buskin River Inn, 1395 Airport Way, tel. (907) 487-2700. 🏨 Pleasant Harbor Lodge, Box 8049, tel. (907) 486-6526; Shelikof Lodge, 211 Thorsheim Ave., tel. 486-4141; Northland Lodge, Box 2376, tel. (907) 486-5578.

Kotzebue

Information: Arctic Chamber of Commerce, P.O. Box 284. **Transportation:** *Air:* Scheduled service from Anchorage via Nome. **Accommodations:** 🏨🏨 Nullagvik Hotel, Box 336, tel. (907) 442-3331; Wien Arctic Hotel, 726 Front St., tel. 442-3160.

Nome

Information: Nome Convention and Visitors Bureau, P.O. Box 251, tel. (907) 443-5535. **Transportation:** *Air:* Scheduled service from Anchorage. **Accommodations:** 🏨🏨🏨 Nugget Inn, Box 430, tel. (907) 443-2323. 🏨🏨 Polaris Hotel, Box 741, tel. (907) 443-2000. *Bed and Breakfast:* Ocean View Manor, P.O. Box 65, tel. (907) 443-2133.

Palmer

Information: Matanuska-Susitna Convention and Visitors Bureau, 191 East Swanson Ave., tel. (907) 376-8001 or Palmer Visitor Center, East Fireweed Ave., open daily May–September, 9:00 A.M.–6:00 P.M. **Transportation:** *Air:* Charter service. *Bus:* Charter service. **Accommodations:** 🏨🏨 Valley Hotel, 606 South Alaska St., tel. (907) 745-3330;

Golden Eagle Motel, 910 South Colony Way, tel. (907) 745-6771. ⏣ Fairview Motel, P.O. Box 745, tel. (907) 745-1505.

Petersburg
Information: Petersburg Chamber of Commerce, P.O. Box 649, open Monday–Friday, 8:00 A.M.–5:00 P.M., May–October; 9:00 A.M.– 3:00 P.M. November–April. **Transportation:** *Air:* Scheduled and charter air service. *Ferry:* Alaska Marine Highway System's southeastern route. **Accommodations:** ⏣ Tides Inn, 1st and Dolphin Sts., tel. (907) 772-4288; Scandia House (historic hotel), 110 Nordic Dr., tel. (907) 772-4281; Beachcomber Inn, P.O. Box 1027, tel. (907) 772-3888. *Bed and Breakfast:* Jewell's by the Sea, 806 Nordic Dr., tel. (907) 772-3620.

Prudhoe Bay
Transportation: *Air:* Scheduled air service and air taxi service. **Accommodations:** ⏣ Prudhoe Bay Hotel, Pouch 34004, tel. (907) 659-2449; Deadhorse Hotel, Pouch 340086, tel. (907) 659-2431. ⏣ South Lake Inn, Pouch 340010, tel. (907) 659-2538.

Seldovia
Information: Seldovia Chamber of Commerce, Drawer F, Seldovia, AK 99663. **Transportation:** *Air:* Charter service. *Ferry:* Alaska Marine Highway System's southwestern route; charter boats also available. **Accommodations:** ⏣ Annie McKenzie's Boardwalk Hotel, Box 72, tel. (907) 234-7816. ⏣ Harmony Point Wilderness Lodge, Box 110, tel. (907) 234-7858; Seldovia Lodge, tel. (907) 234-7654.

Seward
Information: Information Cache, 3rd and Jefferson Sts. (located in historic railroad car "Seward"), open May–September, 9:00 A.M.–5:00 P.M., tel. (907) 224-3094. **Transportation:** *Air:* Scheduled service from Anchorage; charter service; sightseeing flights. *Ferry:* Alaska Marine Highway System's southwestern route. *Train:* Alaska Railroad (to Anchorage, Denali National Park, Fairbanks, and Whittier), tel. (800) 544-0552. *Bus:* Scheduled service to Anchorage. *Car:* Take the Seward Hwy. from Anchorage directly to Seward. *Tours:* Quest Charters (boat trips in Kenai Fjords National Park), tel. (907) 224-3025; Kenai Fjords Tours, Box 1889 MP, tel. (907) 224-3668 or 224-8068. **Accommodations:** ⏣ New Seward Hotel and Saloon, Box 670, tel. (907) 224-8001; Van Gilder Hotel (historic hotel), P.O. Box 2, tel. (907) 224-3525; Marina Hotel, Box 1134, tel. (907) 224-5518. ⏣ Breeze Inn, Box 2147, tel. (907) 244-5237; Murphy's Motel, 4th and D sts., tel. (907) 224-8090. *Bed and Breakfast:* White House Bed and Breakfast, Nash Rd., tel. (907)

224-3614; Korner House Bed and Breakfast, 501 Ash St., tel. (907) 224-3231. *Hostel:* Snow River International Hostel, HCR 64, Box 425, tel. (907) 262-4369.

Sitka

Information: Sitka Convention and Visitors Bureau, P.O. Box 1226, open Monday–Saturday, tel. (907) 747-5940. **Transportation:** *Air:* Scheduled and charter service (airport located on Japonski Island). *Ferry:* Alaska Marine Highway System's southeastern route. **Accommodations:** 🏨 Westmark Shee Atika, Box 318, tel. (800) 544-0970 or (907) 747-6241. 🏨 Sitka Hotel, Box 679, tel. (907) 747-3288. 🏨 Potlach House, Box 58, tel. (907) 747-8611 or 747-8606. *Bed and Breakfast:* Helga's Bed and Breakfast, 2821 Halibut Point Rd., tel. (907) 747-5497; Karras Bed and Breakfast, 230 Kogwanton St., tel. (907) 747-3978. *Hostel:* Sitka Youth Hostel, United Methodist Church, 303 Kimsham St., tel. (907) 747-8356.

Skagway

Information: Skagway Convention and Visitors Bureau, Box 415, tel. (907) 983-2854 or 983-2297; Skagway Chamber of Commerce, P.O. Box 194, tel. (907) 983-2297. **Transportation:** *Air:* Scheduled/ flightseeing service. *Ferry:* Alaska Marine Highway System's southeastern route. Also port of call for cruise ships. *Bus:* Local service. *Tours:* Excursions to Whitehorse on White Pass & Yukon Motorcoaches, tel. (907) 983-2241 or Alaska-Yukon Motorcoaches, tel. (907) 983-2828. **Accommodations:** 🏨 Westmark Inn, P.O. Box 515, tel. (907) 983-2291. 🏨 Golden North Hotel (historic hotel), Box 431, tel. (907) 983-2451 or 983-2294; Skagway Inn (historic hotel), Box 192, tel. (907) 983-2289. 🏨 Wind Valley Lodge, P.O. Box 354-M, tel. (907) 983-2236; Gold Rush Lodge, P.O. Box 514-MP, tel. (907) 983-2831; Sgt. Preston's Lodge, Box 538, tel. (907) 983-2521.

Soldotna

Information: Soldotna's Visitor Information Center (maintained by Soldotna Chamber of Commerce), located in a log cabin on Sterling Hwy., open May– September, Monday–Saturday, 8:00 A.M.–6:00 P.M.; Sunday 9:00 A.M.–5:00 P.M. **Transportation:** *Air:* Charter service. **Accommodations:** 🏨 International Riverside Inn, 44611 Sterling Hwy., tel. (907) 262-4451. 🏨 Soldotna Inn, 35041 Kenai Spur Hwy., tel. (907) 262-9169; Bunk House Inn, 44701 Sterling Hwy., tel. (907) 262-4584; Kenai River Lodge, 393 Riverside Dr., tel. (907) 262-4292. *Bed and Breakfast:* Soldotna Bed and Breakfast, 399 Lovers Lane, tel. (907) 262-4779; Bed and Breakfast on the Kenai River, 245 Binkley, tel. (907)

262-4286. *Hostel:* Soldotna International Youth Hostel, 444 West River-view Ave., P.O. Box 327, tel. (907) 262-4369.

Talkeetna

Information: Talkeetna Chamber of Commerce, P.O. Box 334, Talkeetna, AK 99676. **Transportation:** *Air:* Charter service/flightseeing trips. *Train:* Alaska Railroad. *Tours:* Up River Carriers, Inc. P.O. Box 1488, Talkeetna, AK 99676, tel. (907) 733-2286. **Accommodations:** 🏨 Swiss-Alaska Inn, P.O. Box 65, tel. (907) 733-2424; Talkeetna Motel, Box 115, tel. (907) 733-2323. 🏨 Talkeetna Roadhouse, P.O. Box 388 M, tel. (907) 733-2341; Latitude 62° Lodge, P.O. Box 1478, tel. (907) 733-2262. Papa Bear Lake Lodge, Box 74, tel. (907) 733-2281; Goldilocks Lodge, P.O. Box 300, tel. (907) 733-2741. *Bed and Breakfast:* River Beauty Bed and Breakfast, Main St. and River Park, tel. (907) 733-2741.

Tok

Information: Tok Information Center, Box 359, open daily May–September from 7:00 A.M. – 10:00 P.M.; open Monday–Friday from 8:00 A.M.– 4:30 P.M., October–April, tel. (907) 883-5667. **Transportation:** *Air:* Charter service, flightseeing trips. *Bus:* Summer service to Anchorage, Haines, and Skagway on White Pass & Yukon Motorcoaches and Alaska-Yukon Motorcoaches. *Tours.* **Accommodations:** 🏨🏨 Tundra Lodge, 1315 Alaska Hwy., tel. (907) 883-2291. 🏨 Tok Lodge, 124 Glenn Hwy., tel. (907) 883-2851; Westmark Tok, at junction of Alaska and Glenn hwys., tel. (800) 883-5174 or (907) 544-0907; Snowshoe Gateway Motel, Box 559, tel. (907) 883-4511; Golden Bear Motel, Box 276, tel. (907) 883-2561. *Hostel:* Tok International Hostel, P.O. Box 532, Tok, AK 99780.

Valdez

Information: Valdez Convention and Visitors Bureau, Box 1603-M, tel. (907) 835-4636. **Transportation:** *Air:* Scheduled and charter service. *Ferry:* Alaska Marine Highway System's southwestern route. *Bus:* Scheduled service to Anchorage. *Tours:* Stan Stephens Charters, P.O. Box 1297, tel. (907) 835-4731 (cruises in Prince William Sound and to Columbia Glacier); Alaska Waterways, P.O. Box 1881, tel. (907) 835-5151. **Accommodations:** 🏨🏨 Westmark Valdez, 100 Fidalgo Dr., tel. (800) 544-0970 or (907) 835-4391. 🏨 Village Inn, P.O. Box 365, tel. (907) 835-4445; Westmark Inn, 208 Egan Dr., tel. (800) 544-2206 or (907) 835-4485; Totem Inn, P.O. Box 648 MP, tel. (907) 835-4443. 🏨 Valdez Motel, 136 Egan Dr., tel. (907) 835-4444. *Bed and Breakfast:* The Lake House, P.O. Box 1499, tel. (907) 835-4752; The Garden

House, 708 Cottonwood, tel.(907) 835-2957; Mineral Creek Bed and Breakfast, P.O. Box 1409, tel. (907) 835-5337 or 835-4204; Bed and Breakfast Valdez, Box 442, tel. (907) 835-4211.

Wasilla

Information: Wasilla Museum and Visitors Center, Main St., open Tuesday– Saturday, 10:00 A.M.–6:00 P.M.; Sunday and Monday, noon to 6:00 P.M., tel. (907) 376-2005; Wasilla Chamber of Commerce, P.O. Box 871826, tel. (907) 376-1299; Matanuska-Susitna Convention and Visitors Bureau, 191 E. Swanson Ave., tel. (907) 376-8000. **Transportation:** *Air:* Charter service. *Bus:* Commuter service to Anchorage. *Train:* Alaska Railroad (to Anchorage, Denali National Park, and Fairbanks). *Tours:* Gray Line, tel. (800) 544-2206; Royal Hyway Tours, tel. (800) 647-7750. **Accommodations:** 🏨🏨🏨 Mat-Su Resort, 1850 Bogart Rd., tel. (907) 376-3228 or 376-3229. 🏨🏨 The Silver Fox Inn, Mile 50 Parks Hwy., tel. (907) 892-6179. *Bed and Breakfast:* The Ede Den Bed and Breakfast, Box 870365, tel. (907) 376-2162; Russell's Bed and Board, Mile 37.8, Parks Hwy., tel. (907) 376-7662.

Whittier

Information: City Office, Begich Towers, tel. (907) 472-2327. **Transportation:** *Air:* Charter service. *Train:* Alaska Railroad. *Ferry:* Alaska Marine Highway System's southwestern route. *Tours:* Phillips' Cruises and Tours, tel. (907) 276-8023; Alaska Wilderness Sailing Safaris, P.O. Box 4-275, Anchorage, AK 99509, tel. (907) 338-2134. **Accommodations:** 🏨🏨 Anchor Inn, Box 746, tel. (907) 472-2354; Sportsman's Inn, P.O. Box 698, tel. (907) 472-2352.

Wrangell

Information: Wrangell Convention and Visitors Bureau, Outer Dr., open Monday–Friday, 10:00 A.M.–4:00 P.M. **Transportation:** *Air:* Scheduled and charter service. *Ferry:* Alaska Marine State Highway System's southeastern route. **Accommodations:** 🏨🏨 Harding's Old Sourdough Lodge, P.O. Box 1062, tel. (907) 874-3613; Thunderbird Hotel, 223 Front St., tel (907) 874-3322; Roadhouse Lodge, P.O. Box 1199, tel. (907) 874-2335; Stikine Inn, Box 990, tel. (907) 874-3388.

Yakutat

Transportation: *Air:* Scheduled and charter service available. **Accommodations:** 🏨🏨 Glacier Bear Lodge, Box 303, tel. (907) 784-3202. 🏨 Yakutat Airport Lodge, Box 287, tel. (907) 784-3232.

Index

If more than one page number appears next to the name of a town or an attraction, the boldface number indicates the page where the detailed description appears in the text.